Knowings

Seven Intuitive Principles to a Life of Certainty

By Jill Drader

*Judy Lynn,
Thank you for showing me great leadership, and strength. You know ♡ Jill*

Knowings Copyright © 2024 Jill Drader

All rights reserved. No part of this book may be reproduced by any mechanical, photographic, or electronic process, or in the form of phonographic recording; nor may it be stored in a retrieval system, transmitted, or otherwise copied for public or private use without the prior written permission of the publisher.

Contact Jill Drader jill@jilldrader.com

Editor: Jacquelyn Austin
Cover Artist: Kate Bramley

ISBN 978-1-0688911-1-3   eBook
ISBN 978-1-0688911-0-6   Paperback

First Edition

This is a work of nonfiction.

To all those who helped me see things differently while writing this, thank you!

Contents

Introduction 5
Chapter 1 – Knowings 17
Chapter 2 – The Guides 25
Chapter 3 – Death and Life 33
Chapter 4 – The Nest 43
Chapter 5 – Choices and Change 67
Chapter 6 – The Shadow 83
Chapter 7 – Logic & Intuition 95
Chapter 8 – It's In You 111
Taking it Forward – Finding Your Knowings 121
Appendix 125
    Thank Yous 133
    About the Author 135

Introduction

It's 2020, and I'm unpacking my life again.

Sitting in my new living room on the floor, newly separated, only hours into my new space, I find myself crying while I wait for my food delivery to arrive. I'm glued to my phone app for the doorbell camera that keeps notifying me someone is there, at my old house. It's my ex-husband's new girlfriend moving in beds and couches and big, fluffy pillows and couch throws with her two kids in tow. They are a blended family now.

And me? I am single on my living room floor surrounded by boxes. And Indian food.

I'm unable to stop crying. I've already been diagnosed with PTSD and ADHD, which make me think a little differently. Sometimes expansively, sometimes like I'm spinning. Sometimes I just cry a lot.

My doctor and my psychologist, two of the most important seats on the board of advisors of my life, have recommended I try a new medication that has methamphetamines to calm me down.

Methamphetamines to calm me down?

This counter-intuitive conundrum of the new combo of meds has me confused because, as a person in recovery, I was always told 'absolutely no drugs—abstinence is key.' It's a gentle reminder that I don't know everything.

And, it works, just as they said it would.

I cheated on my psychologist and went to see another because, for a mind like mine, more is never enough. More therapy, more workshops, more self-help books, always more.

Surrounding me are boxes full of memories of my past,

books and books and more books, decor items that just didn't fit in the old house, things I've always wanted to have on a wall in front of me, and a few plants. It's a museum of my past, in boxes and piles around me.

That's how this book came to be. Analyzing books of my past and trying to figure out how I got to be 38 years old and living in my own space, again. Only this time, with little men who spend 50% of their time with me, so I can take care of me the other 50%.

Was rediscovering myself glamorous, like running through a valley after a yoga class? No, because there was no yoga. It was more like crawling out of a deep pit of misery as a result of my choices over a long period of time—sober. It was a lot of staring off into space. A lot of turning seemingly nothingness into wholeness. It was time to own all of that and stand in a new truth.

Because truths change.

It was during this time on my own that I started to do some activities again that I enjoyed but hadn't picked up in a decade. I was eager to get outside and hike, fish, and explore in the Crowsnest Pass. I rooted my path forward in a few values that guided my decision making—adventure, exploration, and self-love. I began to love exploring and adventuring again, going solo to small towns to stop for a cappuccino or $1 books on my way to an Airbnb in a mountain town for a couple days. Most of those towns don't have an espresso machine, and the coffee is really bad, so I stuck to fizzy water as I buzzed around gravel roads to find waterholes and parks.

I couldn't go back to the area where I used to summer. That's where my boys go with their dad now. I needed to find my spot. I needed to find what's for me. In the old mining towns, I'm always fascinated by what's left, what's rotting, and how it feels there. Many feel eerie driving through the Rockies, as rockslides have taken out entire villages over time. While so much is lost and dead at Frank Slide, there's life there if you look carefully.

That's when I found my Knowings, and The OwlSeek Method in Crowsnest Pass.

Introduction

That's when I started fly fishing with Al, another guide and teacher.

That's when he looked me dead in the eye and said, "You need to get some lovin, kid."

He meant that I'd hardened, gotten bitter, and a little resentful. I loved these trips on my own, and longed for the vision to come to reality to do it with someone one day. Someone who loves being outdoors as much as I do.

I went back and forth for months, hiring Al to accompany me up rivers and through forests to sit in silence and fish all day. It was the most comforting thing, and being with him for days at a time really taught me to listen and see things differently.

Then the metaphors started appearing.

The Nest.

The Owl sees you before you see it, as you're out there seeking an answer.

The answer is in the silent wisdom of the Owl within.

The Owl and The Nest are places we must go, knowing that when we get there, that little voice and essence has been waiting for us all along.

I would stay at a quaint BnB where the owner and her daughter would make me breakfast. If I was busy writing, they would bring the meal to my room. Sitting in a room decorated with her grandma's old furniture, I would map out the courses for this thing that was coming to me, and walk the trails to rivers, small lakes, and along railroad tracks in the area.

The methods in this book were downloaded to me during those years when I was back and forth, when my old life ended and I didn't know who I was, navigating the middle of whatever was next. Every time I'd see Al he'd ask about my life, my love life. I would tense up inside, either speaking with shame of some secret hook-up I didn't want my kids to know about, or talking about waiting for what I ultimately wanted to attract.

It was during this time that I found myself again.

I found who I was.

I stepped into what I was called to do.

And before that, I was being human, making mistakes, learning from failures, crying myself to sleep, living in fear, plagued with doubt and uncertainty about what was next.

I found that when I reflected on this method coming to me, it was never complete. No, rather, each thought that came in from the world and each thought created within me was something to cross-check. I was applying it situationally and circumstantially to everything I did, cross-checking which one of the seven data points I was in.

Am I in fear? Am I in 'not able to shift my perspective?' Am I trying to have control? Am I desiring a co-existence?

When I learned how to apply Knowings and OwlSeek, I became more certain of trusting myself to lead my life, co-creating with a source that's too powerful to name that supports what I think, pray for, visualize, and strive for physically and materially. I began seeing everything that happened to me being actually for me, and I could capture the data of my soul in a new way and learn from patterns of nature.

For years I explored for this book, reflecting on old texts referencing the wildness and walking in silence to listen differently to the guided path within, and what to look out for. The signs and clues from that inner whisper also provide guidance, insights, and cautions.

Many people and institutions claim to have the way to this voice, many crossing in and through a man to get there. I'm here to tell you that's not the way. It's in *you*.

When we accept that these truths change, we change. We know a new path forward. A knowing.

This book is not only a collection of my journal entries and lived experiences as I worked to develop a process to move from fear and pride to love and grace, but it is also a guide for accessing your inner knowing in a breath and how to carry it through your career, your relationships, your life.

The Knowings Method is about who we are.

Overall, we will look at Knowings in terms of energy, or connecting to the natural world, and metaphors, meanings,

Introduction

connections, and signs between ourselves and nature—the animal kingdom, or the natural world. We find this throughout history and in texts connecting us to lessons, or stories.

When learning the Knowings Method, it's important to understand that there are different feelings and emotions. At each level, when we become aware of them, we can understand how to get to the next level or learn the next principle.

This is not really about moving through the levels and just completing something; in fact, that won't work whatsoever.

This is about learning and becoming aware of each stage, accepting that we are all of the stages, and that these spiritual principles are what guide our life and unite us.

And understanding that when we become aware of this, we become aware of the nest: the sacred place we go to reflect, and heal, and meditate, and discern, and pray, and listen. When we become aware of the nest, we can become aware of which one of the principles we need to work on in that moment. There's always one.

The point of learning the Knowings program and understanding the flow of the method is understanding that we can take our healing into our own hands and create a sacred, safe space for it. Slowly, we learn that the three highest principles of forgiveness, grace, and love are co-created with a power greater than us, a source we identify when we retreat to the Nest. For some, this source can be their religion or belief system, identified in doctrines and representative archetypes, and it's what they, as an organized group or community, believe and follow. These groups are comfortable coming together and following the same doctrine that may or may not have been passed down, transcribed, and translated many different times since its conception.

The OwlSeek Method is a leadership program, taking us through Knowings' seven spiritual principles to a life of certainty in how we lead. This is for people who want to show up and have a look at where control is creating a miserable life, and maybe not one to be proud of. Sometimes we identify that some of our behaviours are actually manipulative or vindictive; they're coming from a place of wanting retaliation, and acting out vengefully. This doesn't mean that we're actually taking action on our thoughts, but sometimes we catch ourselves in these destructive thoughts that keep us enslaved in this spin cycle of lower vibration more than they help us get out of it.

Having the courage to get out of this spin cycle and truly look at ourselves with a bird's eye view is where we can see where we've become stuck. We have to trust that there's a process that works. The OwlSeek Method is a process that's been tried and tested, and once we get to that place of knowing that there is a different way, we can connect and co-create with something else. So, this can be a new mentor, or a new method, or a new way of looking at how we create strategy, and how we take our ideas and turn them into plans. And we understand that seeing the signs asking us to show up differently is about our own evolution. This evolution means that there's suddenly meaning and purpose in what we're doing, and we're acting from a place that's very intentional. We are inspired by others, and therefore we want to inspire others, and we know we have to let go and surrender what doesn't work. We have to get to a place when we're coming out of the bottom of the spin cycle that identifies what keeps us down there.

This is the depiction on my business card of the one golden tree in the forest. When we get stuck, we're just one tree in the forest, and we're not seeing that golden light inside of us and knowing that we actually do stand out, and we can illuminate a new path. But we know that there needs to be a complete transformation in order to do that. The golden tree on my business card has seven lines that represent the seven principles.

Introduction

Knowings is taking your power back, and is who you are. OwlSeek is aligning your power with calling and skills, and is what you do. The Nest is where you reflect on who you are and what you do.

But first, back to me crying on the floor of my new place surrounded by boxes. I was moving out of my ex-husband's home—the place where our two sons were raised, and where I told him I didn't want to be married anymore. Where I walked into my house and met his new girlfriend/soulmate before I knew she existed. Where I sat by the front window for a decade like a caged bird who couldn't figure out how to get out of the living hell that was my mind. And since I couldn't find my words and my voice to put together a plan, it was put together for me. And now, it was time for me to go.

I felt comfortable in the leaving, and the changing. After decades of chaos in my life, mostly self-magnetized and self-created, I understood the value and the gift in letting go and not knowing what's next. Albeit paralyzing at times, I knew it was happening for me, not to me. And I was scared shitless, mostly walking through the world paralyzed from trying to analyze all the options in front of me. The only thing I knew how to do up until this part of my life was run away. With two kids, I couldn't do the one thing I knew how to do. The one thing I wanted to do. Being almost 40 years old and single, the opportunities to settle were everywhere, but there was also a deep desire in me for change.

There were boxes my parents left me when they moved across provinces years before that I moved from their car to the cellar storage. Never opened, I knew they were filled with old teddy bears, baseball trophies and trading cards, Trolls in Blue Jays jerseys, and dozens of journals. Instead of pulling the books out and putting them into a pile, I opened them one by one, and discovered that the words I wrote to myself then had messages for me now.

They started when I was eight, as a diary—the baby blue one with the pastel teddy bear on the front. The pages are translucent blue, and I wrote in pencil, never staying on the lines. My diary was full of my impending rebellion, where I could tell I was writing so hard I hoped to rip the page. I was writing swear words, like 'My dad is a shit head,' feeling oh-so grown up. I was pushing the boundaries of society and authority in my first decade here on earth.

Through my teens I attached to boys and drugs and false friends, learning codependency as my baseline state and that masks were the way to connect to new people. I wrote of risky behaviours and lies to cover all-night parties, hanging out with older people, and experimenting with chemical drugs, all before I turned sixteen years old. I wrote notes to myself to focus on my education, a concept I didn't grasp until many years later, but somehow always 'just' made it through with lies and excuses and extensions. I didn't actually graduate high school, but I was the organizer of the year-end graduation party and the after-party. I was three credits short, and had to do a correspondence course I mailed in from a beach vacation I took to Costa Rica. I got my diploma in the mail a short time later.

My early 20s were hell on earth fueled by the ball and chain that addiction had on me. I led a complete double life. I was a daily drinker and almost daily cocaine user, and a full-time university student. I was trying to get through school as a normal person, working at a local bar so I could drink while I worked, and exchanging secrets and lies for flaps of cocaine from a local organized crime group who would traffic women from the neighbouring motel. It was then that I saw my first dead bodies as a result of addiction and abuse, at the hands of those who only wished to profit from them. The only way to survive the fucked-up double life that I was living and trying to hide from others was to drink and use and fake that I was ok. With addiction, more is never enough. You need more gambling, more porn, more escorts, more alcohol, more anorexia. I was trying to fake it and manage the craving inside for more. It worked until it

Introduction

didn't work anymore. My rock bottom was a few days of living hell on 'the rock' in South Korea.

My late 20s were for learning how to grow up. I got my first degree in the mail just like my high school diploma. I finally felt like I could be the grown-up wise woman I've always known I was. I would explore and wonder and daydream through putting pen to paper. I've known this from a young age. I've always felt I see the world a little differently from behind my eyes, and in the third eye. I loved to read stories of older women, novels from the library, and biographies of gypsies and mystics and businesswomen, while watching shows I shouldn't watch and listening to the radio shows of "Sex with Sue" under my covers when I was too young.

And, I was.

I learned a lot too young.

Quietly listening and seeing the world around me.

Like when we would break into Mr. Wiener's garage with his daughters to leaf through the milk cartons stacks of Playboy magazines he collected. He drove truck all night and slept all day, so while he was babysitting us, we would sneak into the garage and share a cigarette we stole from him, flipping through glossy pages of naked women. We weren't even teenagers yet and had never touched a boy, but we were training our eyes and minds on how we were to show up when we did.

The journals are the only place where some of my secrets live. During the time I gathering them all together, 65 journals in total—I went through every emotion fathomable flipped through them again—I laughed, I smirked, I felt tantric sex waves, and I cried. I ugly cried. I wailed. I felt my stomach ache and cramp, muscle memory. I felt fear and shame and humiliation alongside pages of love and charity and forgiveness and wonder of the world at large. It brought back memories that I had forgotten. I shuttered at the years of repeating patterns and behaviours and falling in and out of love over and over and not learning terms like boundaries, codependency, and 'not neurotypical' until later in life.

I still, to this day, ask 'why?'

Why were rape and kidnapping and being held at gunpoint for sex and drugs part of my story?

Why were my behaviours while I was addicted to drugs so manipulative?

Why did I betray and hurt good people, really only to hold the hurt and pain in my body for years to come, some even to this day, manifesting as struggle and pain and disease?

Why has the connection to my body with these experiences I went through caused so much pain and scarring and wounding, so much so that my lower abdomen looks like a battleground? Even the tattoo I convinced my parents to let me get at sixteen has moved as I continued to physically grow.

Why, for ten years after having my sons, did my body react so harshly with pain and hemorrhage like bleeding until it was determined at thirty-nine that my uterus must go?

I went to a lot of therapy with Artur and when I thought he was not enough, I would double or triple up the appointments with other specialists to try to fix me, knowing it wasn't what I needed, but not knowing what that might be.

I was always trying to fix something.

Fix what the inner critic was saying was so unlovable in me, highlighting what was wrong with me and how pain-filled my life was. Fix what I was avoiding in my patterns of attraction, desires, lessons, assignments, and revelations. Fix what was, in the end, a spiritual condition.

I didn't know the secret to it all was coming out of the cage and looking at how I show up, and moving to create a space within myself I call The Nest, where I was able to tune into my deepest, most sacred source of healing and wisdom and guidance—my Knowings.

And I wrote about it all, a lot.

I wrote through my confusion.

I wrote through loneliness.

I wrote through abandon and repeated rejection from men.

I wrote about missing my dad.

Introduction

I wrote about disconnection from my mom.
I wrote about illegal things that I was testing society's boundaries on.
I wrote high as a kite, illegible words and abstract doodles after days of no sleep.
I wrote through addiction and obsessive behaviours, some very bad behaviours.
I wrote through abuse, hospitalizations, women's clinics, and overdoses.
I wrote through law enforcement telling me they couldn't help.
I wrote through being too scared to say how I felt, and I could only write.
I wrote through learning I had two selves, a soul self and a shadow self.
I wrote through reflecting on how what I was taught is religion, not faith.
I wrote to spirits and asked for signs, and documented the signs and occurrences.
I wrote to God, and I've written hundreds of letters and prayers to the Universe.
I wrote to God, or god, or spirit, or Universe, or Creator, or the Divine as I changed the names for it.
I wrote asking for help.
I wrote new words like 'manifestation' and 'consciousness' and 'grace.'
I wrote about discernment and trying to figure and feel it all out.
And then I changed.
And then I *saw* life through a higher perspective.
And then I *felt* life through a higher perspective.
And then I *knew* there was a higher perspective. This is the Knowings.

From those journals, I've taken what I discovered as some recurring themes, some findings, some observations, some questions and research, and more questions. I've taken my experiences, and things I've taught others, and put them into this collection of chapters on how to see your journey and story from a different perspective. The Nest.

What if there was a higher perspective to see your inner and higher self?

What if you could learn about it, and then do it over and over, anytime, anywhere?

What if it was your birthright to tune into your breath, and to reset yourself?

What if I could teach you that?

What if I could teach you that writing about yourself *to* yourself is a way to tune into a part of yourself you didn't know existed? Through this place, you can experience a sense of deeper connection and knowing from within, listening to the inner wisdom we all have equal access to. What if I could teach you that you can start here (or complimenting your current journey of talk therapy, counselling, or small group or self-guided inquiry into something you want to know more about), and also teach you how to connect with the right team to help you?

This book is going to teach you, through my lived experiences and studies and research, how to tune into the conscious and unconscious parts of yourself, and turn your negative experiences and thoughts into lessons you can see from a new perspective. See yourself and your story from a different place, applying the Knowings' Seven Principles to move you from being stuck, paralyzed by fear in the cage where you can't make a decision, and feel uncertain, resentful, and withdrawn, to a place of OwlSeek, looking within and co-creating with your higher power to transform your life into one of ease and knowing.

Chapter 1 – Knowings

I was raised around Mennonite communities. My first memory of church was going to a Mennonite church, and they had a very formal religious belief system that I call 'appeasing the grandparents with the section of my closet reserved for Sunday clothes and pantyhose that I can't wear any other day of the week.' Sunday school was a fight every time, not putting on the pantyhose was the only thing that was different. We had to appease the grandparents, and this is like women wear dresses and men don't. The biblical verse, 'Honour thy father and thy mother' is beat into people living a colony lifestyle. In religious control, they refer back to these fear-based verses to discipline, but it is acceptance of abuse and acceptance of brutality, and acceptance of a lot of things under that guise.

Yet, I just love the pacifist nature of loving your enemies, and that violence is never the best way to solve a conflict. And at the same time, closed religious communities become these **doctrines of telling** as the person at the front dictates how it should all unfold—telling the followers in the church, and often those outside of the church, how to live their lives. And so, to appease the person at the front of the church, we fake it to try to fit into this unrealistic formation. But humans don't fit into separate boxes of colonies and churches and other organizations. They make us smaller, and we are here to expand. Today, I drive around rural Alberta near Lethbridge and see all the colonies, and they are still very much doctrines of telling. I go buy eggs and meat from a place where they make the women and children run into the buildings as I pull into the driveway. That's the doctrine of telling, and it is not being, or feeling, or co-creating, or transforming. It is none of the things that I believe are the essence to the conscious path to love.

When I moved to Alberta, I was thirteen years old and my parents had decided they were going to split, which meant no more church. We moved away from the extended family that we were just, in my opinion, going to church to appease.

We came to Alberta and my dad moved back to Ontario to be a pilot. Shortly thereafter, he was flying with Air Canada, so he had to be located there. My mom stayed in Alberta and started a new relationship pretty quickly. Each of my parents have been remarried for twenty-five years. They both found their person, but that transition as a thirteen-year-old is hard when your dad moves across the country, marries somebody much younger, and your mom marries somebody much older. It was a new journey for my brother and myself.

After leaving the only faith I knew and diving deeper into addiction, religion had no place in my life. But after my first year in recovery, I started hearing it differently and even went to Bible College to deepen my practice. I knew there was a deeper, spiritual aspect to all problems, and that a surface-level fix wasn't the answer. I had also found forgiveness at the essence of spiritual life, but wanted to know why I was still angry at religion. I needed to move past the logic of psychology and dive deeper into the spiritual self and deeper knowing.

I understood that forgiveness is co-creation with a higher power or source energy, and once you tap into that grace, a different energy illuminates from within. When you lead with love as a result of forgiveness, you are co-creating with the unknown to feel differently and to lead differently.

Now, let's get clear on some theology terminology. What do you believe? From this point on, I need you to ask yourself if, when God is referenced, does it make you want to run for the door? Are you referencing 'god' with a little 'g' because you believe in several of them? Are you referencing the big boom and the black hole in the stars? Are you referencing aliens? Or does it matter to you which word is used?

Chapter 1 - Knowings

Using different words for source or God goes back to the mystics. It was always the women were rooted in nature. The men went to get commodities and resources, and to fight for land, and to kill. And then it was dominance for empires. Man-made religion is also about dominance and empires. We are now coming back to the only thing missing, which is women's intuition, connection to nature, grounding, and breathing. It is the practice of three deep breaths to connect to the Owl, get into the Nest, and connect to the inner Source of Knowings.

The key piece I want to communicate is to remove all denominations and all man-made religion that creates a tendency to be fake in order to uphold an image for others. My statement of faith is that our soul is our breath. Our breath is gifted to us. We come into the world in a breath. We leave in a breath. Breath. That breath is not ours. That breath is not the body.

Radical, I know.

In my theology studies, nobody would side with me when I said that the breath is soul. This is mostly because Catholicism has created a logic model of 'doing' that's hopped into bed with many western governments to create policy and societal moral compasses to have us believe that giving charitable donations qualifies as 'faith.' Modern day movements like Mormons and Jehovah's Witnesses do this too.

Duty, duty, duty + doing, doing, doing = path to heaven.

I see the breath as a soul connection because we all have it. Breath is the only thing that breaks down the borders of the world, of religions, of needing to associate, of being sober, and of belonging. All we need is to get back to breath and just intuitively connect.

Breath is where logic and intuition meet the problem. We have been living in a logical world, and it's all we know. But what we truly need is quietude and silence to hear our inner self.

For the science-minded:
This is a book about energy.
The energy that is us. The energy that is all around us. The

energy that unites us and divides us. The energy that is quantum physics, epigenetics, biometrics, magic, and miracles.

But this is a book about the source of energy, too.

The source that whispers to each person on earth as to how to access it. The source that is the sun and moon and oxygen that every single human on earth receives. The source that is a higher power of all faiths and religions, the uniting one. The source that is a giver of miracles and spiritual awakenings that keep us saying 'I don't know how' in awe and wonder and mystery.

This is a book about breath, too.

I believe the breath is our soul.

Our soul comes from a source and returns to a source. The same source for everyone. The same soul journey, here now, somewhere else before, somewhere else ahead.

A breath fed by the same trees and leaves that have been here on earth for centuries, as well as those just planted all over the planet today.

In the spirit of journaling, I've asked myself, pen to paper, some questions about the science of energy and breath and soul. Here's what was revealed for the sake of this book.

What is the Source called?

If you can name it, it's not the unseen energy of it.

What does that mean?

Names weaken the power of the energy of it that is unseen, yet felt.

What do people call it?

God, Creator, Universe, Allah, Love, Jesus Christ, Christ Energy, Jehovah, Yahweh, or hundreds of other names ...

Is Love an energy?

Yes, it is the greatest energy of all.

Who says?

Each belief and faith and organized religion talks about the essence of the same thing.

Everyone can tap into it and feel it. That is, until they think too much about it, then it's lost.

Chapter 1 - Knowings

Is love the only energy?
No, but it's the most important one to start with.
What are other energies?
Grace, Forgiveness, Intuition, Courage, Pride, and Fear.
What else is energy?
Music, Art, Feelings, Tears, Hugs, Births, Deaths, Anger, Actions, Prayer, Consequence.
Are cults energy? Quilting groups? Hockey teams?
Yes. Yes. Yes.
Grief circles? Funeral homes? Intensive Care Units and Emergency Rooms?
Yes, they are where you live or die, or live through dying, or die a certain soul death trying to survive.
Are thoughts, beliefs, and actions also energy?
Yes. Yes. Yes.
Is science about energy?
Yes. It's about testing the hypothesis of the seen and the unseen.
Is spirituality about energy?
Yes. It's about testing the feelings of the seen and the unseen.
Are religions about energy?
Yes. Religion is about witnessing as a collective through theories as described by the doctrines.
Are they the same energy?
Yes.
With the same outcomes?
No.
Why?
Humans have thoughts. Humans have free will. People, mostly men, focused on power by controlling thoughts for a long time, creating cages within cages.
Is perspective also energy?
I think so. It's free will.
Everything is energy. If you can feel it, see it, taste it, sense it, or think about it—it's energy. Things we think become things, thus making it a transfer of energy of a thought to a thing. The

power of that transfer is the movement of energy. We can't see energy, can't microscope it, yet we can all agree there is something to it.

Are souls energy?
Yes.
How?
Breath.
And spirits?
Yes.
How?
They're like thoughts. You can't see them, but they are energy.
Spirits and souls are energy that we can't see?
Yes.
What about energies of dark places?
That's up to you.
What about energies of light places?
That's up to you, too.
Why?
People listen to someone else and take the energy of what they hear and make it their own truth, and that has an energy to it.
Do they change?
Yes.

It's the energy of states of minds. Collective or divided, energy can make people rise, or fall, together. It's the miracles, the 'I don't know hows,' the spiritual awakenings, and the enlightened states. It's the energy of connection of the spiritual world here on earth and on the other side.

What's the other side?
That's up to you.
What if there is no other side?
That's up to you, too.
For the religious-minded:

Jewish believers of the Old Testament believe one type of heaven. Christians, who believe the Old Testament and the New

Chapter 1 - Knowings 23

Testament, believe in another kind of heaven. Believers of Jesus are now thousands of denominations that have broken down different rites and ways and traditions that lead you there. New Thought Christians believe in a heaven and other places the spirit and angel worlds are, which is a more spiritual take of feeling the Holy Spirit. Muslims, believers of Islam, believe in a heaven and a hell where judgment on your deeds and how you obeyed and lived will determine where you go. The righteous go to *Janna* (heaven).

Hinduism believes in the ultimate destination of Moksha or Nirvana, but first you are reborn many times according to your karma, a heaven of sorts, and Naraka is a place to go, like hell, if you need to relearn your lessons before your next life.

Buddhists believe in *sagga,* where you are reborn, or enjoy life after death for your past skillful actions, accumulated merits, and good deeds, is a heaven of sorts. You are not punished in any way—that's a Western belief.

They all speak of wanting to be saved, the same thing, the same place, the same pathways to try to live more good than bad. They all speak of trying to live more righteously and serving your neighbours while having faith, and listening.

Listening is what we all experience differently.

Some listen through man-made repetitive words, phrases, verses, rituals, and rites.

Some listen in silence.

Some listen in spaces where the spirit moves through wildly.

Some listen using idols and objects to support the journey.

Some use prayer beads, rosary, candles, scarves, prayers, and pillows to sit upon.

Some use chants to say verses from books, rituals, and traditional repetitions of prayers.

Some blend faith and science, a metaphysical world of sorts.

Some use logic and soul, and I think we've lost this part of ourselves, our knowing. I think the wisdom book and the ancient texts and the mystics of the past were all talking about the same thing, and it's been lost in the noise of the world.

Some talk about the psychological components of the conscious, subconscious, and psyche parts of ourselves and how they have come together to formulate our beliefs today, influenced by our environments.

I think we need to examine our collection of thoughts, and ask ourselves—is this true? Is this a fight worth fighting? And what if things change?

We are all using different language talking about the same things, and the same places.

How do I know this?

The greatest teacher I ever had taught me.

Chapter 2 – The Guides

Ms. Baxter
I don't remember how the invitation happened.
    I only remember that it felt like it was right, but also wrong.
    It was wrong because I was only sixteen and I was going to a teacher's house, and I hadn't asked my parents. I didn't know what I was going for, but I knew that if I asked my parents, they would probably say no. She told me to come for 10 a.m. on a Saturday.
    The house was different from the other houses I knew.
    It was an end unit townhouse, connected to the one beside it.
    I was raised in a farmhouse, then a house in a small town, then a house in a bigger town. I don't recall having ever been in a townhouse before that day, and the levels were curious to me.
    Ms. Carolyn Baxter greeted me at the door smelling of stale cigarettes and something else, something stronger, like vodka.
    We walked up the first set of eight stairs to her kitchen. She was sipping something translucent straight on ice, in a short glass. *But it's only 10am. But you don't serve water like that.*
    I was there for a reading. She sat me at the kitchen table and asked if I wanted water.
    There was a business card on the table in front of me. It read:

H.U.G.S Unlimited
"The Greatest Journey… is the Journey Within."
Carolyn Baxter
B.Ed., Grad. Diploma
Professional Speaker
Transformation Consultant

Her address and phone number were also on the card, and her address was in a neighbourhood I had always wanted to live in as a kid, Woodacres. Woodacres was where the big houses were. I lived in Wood Valley where the houses were average. We could have never afforded a Woodacres address when I was younger.

I was in awe of the windows in her kitchen, and it seemed her cat and dog loved the light that came through. It overlooked Fish Creek Park, a wall of pine trees in front of a clear, blue sky. The sun was coming in hot and bright. Magpies, blue jays, and geese flew by the windows.

There were stacks of cards on the table. Not playing cards, but cards with symbols on them that said something about Egypt and angels. I had never seen cards like them before. Tarot? Oracle?

In high school, she was my psychology teacher for two years. When she walked down the hallway, students parted like the Red Sea. She had a presence, a boldness, and there was something about her voice. It scared others, but I was drawn to it. It was deep and raspy, probably from years of smoking. She was the only teacher that would come out to the 'smoke pit' near her parked car, and smoke back-to-back cigarettes during recesses and lunch breaks. She'd put one high heel on her running board and lean on her open door, smoking without a care in the world with underage kids standing in the smoking section designated by a yellow circle painted on the ground.

But she taught in a more feminine way, full of wisdom, and could scare the shit out of you at the same time if you didn't know how to hear this voice. We would do meditations for some classes. I thought she was just trying to take a break herself when she would dim the lights and tell us to put our heads down with our eyes closed. She would start a cassette tape of some twinkly wind chime music and walk us through a meditation. Half of us were stoned from smoking a joint for lunch, myself included, and did not take it seriously. However, years later, this one practice has become one of my most valuable tools to calm my central nervous system. It is also what I regularly teach others. She started shuffling the cards on the table, talking about things I didn't know—tarot, past lives, intuition, angels, oracle, communicating with angels, Spirit, transformation, and goddess energies. She spoke of conscious and subconscious states, words I spelled wrong in my journal when I later reflected on the experience.

We started with past life regression stories of who I was in past lives and how I was connected to people. There were visions of lives lived, lives lost, lessons learned, and lessons not learned that carry through to next lifetimes. She said my mom and I lived in a Greek fishing village, and our husbands were fishermen, and we were friends who helped each other see what we wanted out of life. She said my dad and I lived through the French Revolution together. She said my brother and I were twins in Europe when our parents died when we were about nine and we went on the road becoming musicians together to make money until he settled down with a nice girl, and I travelled and became a barmaid who never had children. She said she and I were together in the Middle Ages and she was a spiritual guide and psychic, but I never listened to her, and that's why our souls were back together here, in this time, now.

She believed in one monotheistic God, one source, one energy that is the Spirit of the source of life for all of us. We all have access to it, we all are connected to it, and we can all learn and grow from it. This was all something she understood years before I learned to connect to higher energies to take a higher perspective and get out of the cages that we create for ourselves.

She was called to teach me, her student, some of the language that would become my natural lexicon years down the road. She knew there was alignment for me to know her. It was a magical kind of connection, and a curious one—she was a woman in her fifties and I was sixteen, but there was a knowing, a knowing we were meant to connect, and that I would need it. The kind of faith she connected me back to was not something I could have found on my own in the environment I was in, a kind of faith that kept me alive when my hands and legs were bound and I couldn't escape, powerless at the harmful hands of another.

As I mentioned earlier, there was no spiritual component to the religion I was raised in. It was more of a telling. When my parents moved away from it, I was certain I didn't want religion, but I did think about there being more out there. These things always caught my eye, like new-age displays of crystals and suncatchers in windows, books in the library on topics too mature for me to understand, but were intriguing.

In the short time Carolyn was in my life, she made herself known to be the greatest teacher I've ever had, and still is. I don't hesitate for a second to admit that I don't understand what I understand, because that is the awe of what God and the Universe and Source Energy does—it aligns people and places and situations to have profound impacts on each other in this lifetime.

We prepare each other.
We warn each other.
We share with each other.
We teach each other.

The seeds were planted in me to listen to an inner voice, feel things around me that I couldn't see, or tap into on my own, or learn from anyone else. She is a Divine God-Send. She was sent to me to show me another way to teach others what I was shown.

Until she died, and things changed.

Chuck

I met a man in recovery. This was 2007, my first year in recovery, and he was chairing a recovery meeting. I'd just moved back from Korea, and he said he was a Korean War vet. For the next nine years, we became friends. He called me twice a day. He was a grumpy old dude, and nobody liked him. He was inappropriate. I constantly told him, "You can't say that!" He spoke like it was still the 70s and 80s, but I felt called to just walk with him.

Chapter 2 – The Guides

He was never married, never had kids. He said his mom died at childbirth. One time, he had to go to the hospital for a hernia operation, but he was so scared of the hospital. He lived in the same apartment at Eight and Eight for thirty-five years. And he did the same routine every day, including three meetings for recovery. Every day, he was in bed by 5:30 p.m. and up at 4:30 a.m. He never had cable, and only listened to CBC radio.

I took him for the Doctor's appointment because he was in pain, and I said I would accompany him. That's a service part of the recovery world, which is about getting out of yourself and your selfishness. Sometimes it's offering coffee to people, volunteering your time, or helping people move. But you have to be careful that you don't start over-helping and over-giving and using it as a sense of ego. When I brought Chuck to his appointment, he put me down on paper as his only next of kin.

Then one day, for the first time in five years, I don't hear from him. No calls. I don't hear from him the next day either, and I can't get a hold of him. I called the apartment manager first and he said he couldn't do anything, so we called the police, asking for a wellness check. I followed them into Chuck's apartment. He was in the fetal position in bed and he didn't want to go in the ambulance. He said he would only go if I drove him.

The police load him in my car, and I turn on my voice recorder and he says, "Jill, the painting of the clouds on the wall opened up and they said I'm wanted in heaven, and then they show that you drive me to the hospital and I never get out."

I'm on the recording, saying, "Oh it's okay, Chuck. Let's just go get this checked out. You probably just need to get some medication, or a specialist."

We get into the ER and eventually the doctor brings me the X-ray and shows me the darks spots on the illuminated image. He says Chuck has cancer in every single organ and we should have detected this years ago. He's not leaving the hospital. I have Elizabeth Gilbert's book, *Big Magic*, in my hands. That was the book I had started, and it's all about knowing, and so I sat there with him knowing this wasn't good. He went from diagnosis to death in four months, and died in my arms. He never went back home. And because he wrote it on a piece of paper years before, I was the person to make all of the end-of-life decisions for him.

I suddenly had no work, and I had my sons full-time because of a childcare issue, and I was walking this man to the end of his life. My pictures from those three months are of my sons in the palliative care unit with us because I had to go every day until I held him in the Sarcee Hospice for his last breath. And if you hold somebody in hospice for their last breath, you know when the soul leaves the body.

Chuck was unconscious when we transferred him from Peter Lougheed to Sarcee Hospice. He had a heart attack and slipped off the bed. I've never seen somebody have a heart attack and actually look like that. What I saw was something out of *The Exorcist* movie, like the body was flailing.

A guy from high school who was in Ms. Baxter's class came in as the EMT for the transfer, so I felt okay that I would meet them at the hospice. When we got there, there was a dim lamp on beside the bed and pot lights, and Chuck opened his eyes and said, "Turn off the light," and then, "Turn that one on."

He hadn't spoken in days. I wondered, *You want the really bright fluorescent light on?* and I told myself, "Just do it." He rolled towards pot light, and he went exactly like he said he would. The clouds in the picture opened up and it was so great.

I was driving home past Rockyview General Hospital, and I felt an embrace from behind me and a voice said "Thank you for bringing my baby home." Then I hit the curb. I actually thought somebody was in the car, and that's how I know there is spirit and soul. Because I have felt it. I have heard it. And I've seen it.

Artur

I took this to Artur, my psychologist. We have been working together since 2015, and Artur might be the only person in my life to know most of my story. Well, not my whole story, but most of it. There's still stuff I'm ashamed to tell anyone. He is

Chapter 2 – The Guides

the only person I have found a way to open up to that helps uncover what I really need to say and where that's coming from within. (It's usually the one-liners that he leaves me with.)

The knowing I have and the place it comes from is deep, and it's wise. It's not understood by everyone, but he understands.

He's been the voice of questions, reason, challenge, support, encouragement, understanding, and sometimes he just shakes his head in silence, the kind of presence I need. If I could afford to see him weekly, I would.

'Odd Duck' is how I've been described by others and something Artur would say, "isn't exactly wrong." In his Eastern European accent laced with lived experience, wisdom, religious understanding, and a careful approach to traditional psychology and pathology, he was right.

And my ex-husband was right. I am an odd duck. And I locked myself in a cage I didn't want to be in. My perspective had dimmed so dark that I was a bird flocking with no one, alone in my cage.

My soul and inner desires were screaming for more, and on eagle wings is the only way I could imaging myself soaring out of where I was to where I want to be.

Artur has helped me learn to open the cage from the inside out, and with that comes a kind of transformation, a change. If the right person can ask the right questions, the soul and the mind and the body can go through changes of all sorts—like a caterpillar to a cocoon to a butterfly.

I am an odd duck. While I value the flocks and communities around me, I will always walk a little bit of a different walk, and that's ok. While I didn't connect with those around me very much, I did connect with who I was within me.

There's not one way.
There's not one truth.
They've been tainted.

There's not one way, but the right person can ask the right questions for you to discover your way, and that is my hope with this book for you. It starts the conversation with yourself to align with your Artur (counsellor, therapist, psychologist, or psychiatrist) once you do a deep dive into yourself with some inquiry and journaling. You're also going to need some new teachers, either physical people you listen to, or people who have passed whose words are still vibrating off the lips of many in a positive, or positively critical way.

There is more than we know. Artur keeps me curious.

As a student coming out of high school, I took a couple years off to 'find myself' and run around Europe, India, Costa Rica, and Western Canada.

It turns out that 'myself' wasn't there, but I found something else, and that's a lot of questioning of what I was told is 'truth' and 'true' growing up. There is a ceiling to academics and scientific thinking that I was taught up until that point, but I didn't know that before.

Things change.

People change.

We change.

And that's ok. You can change your mind, too.

To investigate your inner world, you have to find some data to analyze from your soul. You can do this by going within and meditating and listening, or you can write (journal) to yourself.

Chapter 3 – Death and Life

I have experienced death in so many ways in my life, I can't even begin to count them. Death of an illusion, death of a marriage, death of a business, death of an addiction, and the rebirth that followed. We can choose to stay in the cage of death, or we can choose a different perspective and use the compost for new growth.

When I was learning from Ms. B, I was in high school and I wasn't interested in the park behind her house for any other reason than to sneak down with friends to drink 40 oz beers, smoke joints, and stay later than closing time. 'Adventure' to us was running away from park rangers after dark who were mad at us for not putting out our fires and behaving badly, as they should have been. We were in rebellion.

From fourteen years old on, drugs and alcohol seeped into my life, and the clarity and connection to the things she taught me got foggy. Until I turned twenty-four, I was clouded by substance use and abuse, ballooning into a full-blown addiction. I moved far away from the things she tried to teach me in those years, on the dark side of the world where I lost control and became powerless.

Sometimes I think she knew; she just knew that I was on this path and she needed to get to me before I almost drank myself to death too. See, her death shaped me, and gave a boundary of sorts in my using, and she taught me a phrase that never left me: "We aren't powerless, but we give our power away."

I needed that when I entered a drug treatment program (for the third time before I turned twenty-one), and the first thing we talked about was powerlessness. What she told me reminded me that I had it in me, I just forgot or moved away from it or had given it away. I had thrown away the key to the cage.

And I had another knowing.

I could take my power back. I could move myself out of the fearful life I was living, and I could turn another way. I could walk through a process of taking a real hard look at myself with a bird's eye view—but that was just one perspective, and if I stayed there, I stayed spinning in the past, which is depression. I could also shift my perspective and come down from that view and find the Nest, a centre of sorts. I could adopt a new perspective looking at the tree from beside it, not looking down on it.

When this realization happened, everything changed, for me, and those who were called to teach with me.

The Obit

I had just returned from a backpacking trip in Gujarat, India. I went to my parents' coffee shop, Jungle Java, and opened the daily paper, The Calgary Sun. Flipping through, likely looking for the horoscopes, I landed on the Obituaries page.

And there she was.

A picture of her shining soul with her dog on her lap.

Ms. Baxter was dead.

I called two friends from high school who aligned with her teachings, Mitch and Ryan, and the three of us went to her funeral. They were musicians who connected to an energy and source through music, something I couldn't understand, but she could. Each of us had our quirks. Mitch was getting into modeling and tattoos, and Ryan worked with his family, renovating and painting houses.

I saved the Celebration of Life pamphlet from her funeral. It has a picture of her on the front, the only picture of her I have that's not the obituary. I've had it pinned up in my kitchen for the last two years so she can oversee her old place, and whisper words of wisdom to me from the other side.

On the back is this poem, some words she left for me to

Chapter 3 – Death and Life

ponder and really feel into what is on the other side. What is death? Where do you go? Which faith is right?

Death is Nothing at All

Death is nothing at all.
It does not count.
I have only slipped away into the next room.
Nothing has happened.

Everything remains exactly as it was.
I am I, and you are you,
And the old life that we lived so fondly together is untouched, unchanged.
Whatever we were to each other, that we are still.

Call me by the old familiar name.
Speak of me in the easy way which you always used.
Put no difference into your tone.
Wear no forced air of solemnity or sorrow.

Laugh as we always laughed at the little jokes we enjoyed together.
Play, smile, think of me, pray for me.
Let my name be ever the household word that it always was.
Let it be spoken without an effort, without the ghost of a shadow upon it.

Life means all that it ever meant.
It is the same as it ever was.
There is absolute and unbroken continuity.
What is this death but a negligible accident?

Why should I be out of mind because I am out of sight?
I am but waiting for you, for an interval,
somewhere very near,
just round the corner.

All is well.
Nothing is hurt; nothing is lost.
One brief moment and all will be as it was before.
How we shall laugh at the trouble of parting when we meet again!

–Henry Scott Holland

It was hereafter that I started to connect with her on a soul level. While she was gone, we were the same. Our conversations were still being had. Her guidance was still around me. So I continued to keep talking to her, and twenty years later these are the words that have come from this reflection of how she keeps showing up for me, guiding me, teaching me, and writing this with me.

Death
Nothing in the forest lives without the forest dying.
A kind of necessary death.
A kind that is new life.
A kind that is regenerative.
A kind that is helpful to keep those here well.

Death is the absolute heart and centre to everything, because we're comfortable with living, and we're comfortable with death being this thing over here that we don't know about, but think we don't need to know about. It's easy to turn your back to it.

But on this notion of it being a pendulum between love and fear, life and death, we find death and fear at the same place.

The death is death of a dream, death of an idea, death of a way of thinking, death of an expectation, or death of some object—an inanimate object, like if a building burns down, or a business you have to close down. But we only associate 'death' with the death of a person.

Chapter 3 – Death and Life 37

We address death in those three days after. We take a casserole over, and then just try to get through the funeral. And then just like death happens, we come and we go. But we all need to think deeper about death.

Most people fear their relationship with death and have an absolute fear of death. They don't want to take the mask off, or go into the ego. The reason why they don't want to surrender is that it could be telling them something meaningful, or it could have a message for them.

It could be that big unseen, unknown, curious piece about the other side. What happens after we die? Most people have an absolute fear of that. And until they see the signs that there's a new perspective, there's another way, fear will always be our lens.

I had a client last week who shared, "My grandpa died, and everybody in the family says he came through to them, even my sister's son. When is he going to come through to me?"

I replied, "He's there. He's never not been there like that. He doesn't die with the death. That connection is still alive. You have to know; you have to watch for the signs." Being able to get to the other side of death is where you find forgiveness, grace, and love.

Many Little Deaths

Walking alongside Chuck to his death was one of the biggest journeys of my life. I didn't know what I was doing. I'd had the biggest collapse in my life. It was July 2015. Three things happened during the first week of that month. This is ten years after I got sober, and I had a digital platform called "Women in Work Boots." It was used across Canada and I received awards for it.

The digital platform got hacked by male body enhancement ads, and then was firewalled from the 200 schools it was being used in.

We had been using international students as nannies. I'd been a nanny myself in Italy and in France during university, and I wanted that in my house. I wanted people who spoke Spanish so

I could become more fluent. I wanted people who spoke French so I could remember all the French I knew. It was a great arrangement for our family. And then after eight girls I said, "You know, I'm in this world of gender stigma stamping within construction. Why don't we get a male nanny from the same agency with an early childhood education background? These guys had mountain bikes and hockey on their profiles and my two sons could shoot 10,000 pucks a day and still want more. Everyone would have a great time.

We chose a nanny, and he was good fit for a year. That was, until we learned he had been photographing me without my knowledge in the bathroom and when I was changing in my bedroom.

I caught him out at the house at the lake. I was getting out of the pool, and I saw a DSLR lens in the bottom corner of the window frame. I screamed and ran to the window. All I saw was an extended shadow of something running away. I couldn't tell if it was male or female, but I saw the shadow run away.

Then I went upstairs to talk to Tyler about it. There were only the two of us and the male nanny on this thirty-acre property out in the Shuswap. And he then came back with his camera. He said he was photographing the sunset and told me that he hadn't taken any pictures of me. My third eye chakra started pulsing. When I had the thought, 'Did he do it?' it pulsed, and when I went away from the thought, 'Could he be telling the truth?' it stopped. I realized that when I was thinking truth statements, it pulsed, and it did this through the night.

In the morning, he confessed that it was him. He'd photographed me through the window. He was so sorry, and he deleted everything, but we sent him home from there, and put him on a bus back to Calgary. My mom and brother packed up his room in Calgary, and a courier met him with his bags at the airport.

I went to see a psychic after, because I could not even be in my own house, and the psychic told me that we hadn't cleaned everything out of his bedroom. The reason I couldn't be in my

Chapter 3 – Death and Life

house was because there was a shoebox with an external hard drive in it, which ended up having images of me from before that he had taken in the house.

I had to put to death this idea that it was this great experience, but I also had to put to death this idea that I was healed, and everything was great on the other side. I wasn't. I was just starting.

So, after my digital platform had to be shut down because of hacking, and we had to let go of our nanny for secretly filming me, Chuck was diagnosed with cancer.

These three things in my life showed up as a death of the idea—the way that I thought life was going, and the trajectory I thought I was on.

The way I really wanted to get through it was to control, force, fear, and project my ego to make everything okay. I had to step out of this place where we want to stay stuck, and not deal with death, and not deal with the living death.

Now I share the new process of death like a Death Doula, where instead of helping through birth you are helping people through death. You walk with them because it's so scary. Eventually, you have to have the courage to shift and surrender what your ideas were, and then trust that it's trying to teach you something.

Because through connection, transformation, and leadership, we evolve to co-create with something else that we could find in life. In this, we change and transform and know the difference between being stuck and in a place of fear, versus being liberated and living in leadership and living in this powerful place where we're illuminating from within. When we illuminate from within, our life and death pieces are balanced.

In my life, in my journals, and now in this book I am sharing many little (and some significant) deaths. Ms. Baxter died, I had to die off a part of myself in addiction, and so on.

If you choose to live in the cage, you're shutting down. This idea of being stuck in any aspect of your life is really staying in a fear-based place, like a living hell.

Death is necessary.
Nature is a great example and has all these seasons of death. Things kill each other off in the circle of life. In the hidden life of trees, the root systems connect and if these trees feel another tree is bringing a threat of disease or weakness to their group, they'll snip off the roots and kill them at the source, which is what we're doing tribally with land, thus modelling patterns of nature.

We don't have healthy soil unless we have death. Nothing in the forest regenerates without death. And we need to look at those patterns in ourselves with everything we're living in relationship with.

Some of you might be going through it in your relationship—facing the idea that a relationship has to die instead of the idea of carrying somebody 'until death do us part.' Some of these man-made, antiquated ideas also have to die.

Sometimes death is about the death of addiction, and a life that caused so much strife, pain, and suffering on those around us. When my friend Bruce Oake died, I received the horrific call from the coroner in the middle of the night. I was told they called me before his parents. Bruce always wanted me to meet his mom, Anne, and when we did meet at Indigo bookstore in Dalhousie, it was to discuss his passing. Bruce always said I was like her. He said I would like her. And I did. So much I didn't want her to see me cry, so I excused myself to the bathroom and prayed to Bruce to give me a sign he knew I finally met her. When I got back to the table, she was crying. A book on the shelf behind her fell. Its title was Bruce. Anne said she felt a sign from him to let me know he knew I was there. Sadly, Anne passed a few years after Bruce, yet her dream of a treatment centre in Winnipeg was born before she passed, the Bruce Oake Recovery Centre. She had a dying dream too, a women's centre that is now in the fundraising stage to one day become a reality.

Sometimes death is about the death of a mindset, death of a hierarchal, patriarchal system created that we're told we have to be in, and instead it's about living in the new. My office is filled

Chapter 3 – Death and Life

with plants that are all sprouting and living in water. There are ways to get to new life and it doesn't have to only be in soil. It doesn't have to only be in water either, as some plants are air plants. We can all find new ways to grow.

Rebirth in the breath

Death is in everything. Every religion has a death doctrine. Some spiritual beliefs also take the transfer of energy into account. Energy can't be created or destroyed. It can only be transformed.

I am working to transform our habits of forcing toxic positivity on death (or the opposite response of fear and resistance) so that we all see it as a way of the world, and surrender and shift and realize it's going to change us.

Most of the times Jesus spoke to people, it was when he was leaving them with a question so they could reflect on the answer within—asking them to reflect on a death of sorts, death of an idea or mindset.

In the breath after a death, you feel a shift to knowing that you are different and you're seeing things differently. Then you see death through the eyes of love and living.

Death comes to help show us that we don't have to fear it. It's where logic and intuition meet. It keeps the pendulum swinging naturally. It's the toxic positivity of "Everything's great. Love, love, love! Push through and focus on positive things" versus "I'm too scared. Fear it, don't go there, shut it down, turn your back to it." Death just stays as this dark thing, but it's not. It's this life-giving dark thing, but we have to shine light on it, and we have to bring illumination from within to anything that appears dead.

Chapter 4 – The Nest

Allow me to share why and how birds became symbols for the Knowings process.
 In order to survive, birds must adapt to their surroundings. If they don't adapt, they risk extinction. Adaptations are having results of the environment that they live in or are migrating to. You can't take a parrot from the Caribbean and hope it survives in the wild in the Canadian North. It won't. It would take time and a slow acclimatization if it were to happen. It means that if they can adapt, the result is going to be positive to their future success. If they don't adapt to environmental change, they lose their ability to hunt for their basic needs, like food and shelter. I think this is why I'm so attracted to birds. Why, in quiet observation, they always stand out to me. And I think this is also why I'm able to understand why so many people fear them.
 Birds are swift. They move consciously, they move quietly, or they squawk loudly. Sometimes they are an annoyance or an intrusion to the environment. I, however, like to sit back and just watch. The pictures in my kitchen of a Great Horned Owl, and a Bluebird, and a Blue Jay remind me every day to tune in to some of the meanings that I've associated with them drawn from various myths and faiths and stories and traditions, and I'm able to very carefully and sacredly craft the impact and the meaning for me. I think in this time of looking for signs and being careful not to analyze too much, we can get lost in the middle of attaching on to somebody else's idea or meaning of what it is.
 I see a lot of people who don't align with or reject the faith that they were raised in, and they move towards more of the Indigenous, or natural creation stories. In some of this, I see

strong attachments to some of the meanings that come up, and I'm always curious how people hold on to one thing when really, in the world, we can observe so many things.

To me, the Blue Jay represents a kind of messenger. It has this powerful presence and if animated, it looks like the bird that would deliver me a letter. I see Blue Jays when I am really stuck in my logic place, and I'm overthinking, and it's like they appear to remind me to soften a little bit, and that I can wrap up my thoughts and move on. I find them to come and go quickly. Sometimes I can't even see their flight path, they're so quick. Where I live, they really blend in with the sky, so as soon as they leave the dark green trees, I lose them in the clouds.

I have connected to the Bluebird in a very sacred, special way. The Bluebird first came to me as my assignment as Ms. Baxter was back in my life, and I called my first intuitive business 'Divine Blue Bird' when I started to feel signs from her. One sign came through the two Blue Jays that came to visit me when I was asking for a sign if I should get the townhouse that was in direct view of her old house. Another time, a divine Bluebird came as I was ready to tee off in Waterton on the back nine, on the fourteenth hole I think, and it was about three feet in front of me and just hovered there, as though it was trying to tell me something.

It was there long enough that I couldn't go through with my shot, and I had to wait. I looked back to see if my two friends also noticed it was there, and they did. It was somewhat of a miracle moment, and none of us had seen this bird anywhere in this environment or on the course before and my friend, an avid golfer who spends her summers there, also had never seen one. We've actually seen more grizzly bears on the course than that bird since the park burned down years ago.

Birds really came to life for me when I made them into archetypes, or meanings, for the different areas between this program. I find birds to be a nice association to each one of the stages here, as everyone globally can connect with the kind of bird, or one similar to it, from their environment. It's one of those unique things we can all relate to.

Chapter 4 – The Nest

Every day, I have coffee at the same time that Ms. Baxter was probably pouring her first vodka. I called one of her former Spiritual Life Centre students while researching for this book. She confirmed that Ms. Baxter drank a 26 oz bottle a day, probably at school while teaching me—but no judgement. I was high too.

Everyday I sit and think about where she is now, and how I still feel her presence. Every single day, I think about the seeds she planted for me to discover, teaching me of angels and messengers of light and God. It seems like I'm talking to her in my head, and there's also a knowing that I'm connecting to her on another level.

Sometimes I talk to her out loud.

Sometimes I feel her around me. Other times, I doubt what I know is true.

See, I know she's there, even though she's not there.

I know she hears me, even though she's not here to hear me.

I know she advises me, even though I hear her through a different channel.

I know she loves me, because I feel it.

I know she feels it when I say 'thank you' or 'I love you.'

I call this place where she and I met, 'The Nest.'

The Nest is a place within us. It's in me, and it's in you. We have all been gifted access to the Nest with the first breath we were given when we came to birth here, and we leave it in this body of ours in the last breath we take here on earth. The Nest is this life we've been given.

Knowings is a remembering, a reminder of where we came from, and the source of the whispers in the Nest. Those cautionary feelings of warning come from this source. No matter the faith or belief systems people choose to believe, the Knowing is at the heart of each one. That source of inner love and protection when you're all alone and something says 'Just keep going'—it's that.

In the Nest, everyone has access to this inner source or higher power—there's no cage or key. It's where we have access to all of the sources of energy, light, knowing, and wisdom. It's where we can ask unseen things for support and strengthen our Knowing muscle.

OwlSeek is a journey on how to communicate more clearly and concisely with our inner self, the place where subconscious thoughts are formed, and conscious thoughts are considered.

Intuition and logic are here to work together, like our soul self and our ego self. It's where your logic informs your Knowing, and Knowing trumps logic. It's where we create imaginary locks and keys with our mind, and our logical fear-filled selves. We put people in place who lead groups of people or societies or religious movements and we give them the power to have the key to open it for us, and that's giving away our own access to the higher, inner gifts and noticings we all have.

The Nest is where we leave things we are done with and need to release, need to let go, need to surrender, and need to ask for help opening the cages we've locked parts of ourselves in.

See, nests aren't cages.

Cages are constructs of our minds. Nests are the quiet sanctuaries of our hearts.

Nests are purposeful, intentional, and necessary.

Nests are personal.

Nests are safety, shelter, nurturing, for birthing.

Nests are for giving life, and for releasing back into the wild.

Nests create new life, and sustain life.

Nests are sometimes where things in life come to an end, too.

Nests are for rest, and sometimes long sabbaticals.

Nests are for retreats. Nests are for Knowings.

The Knowings Method is about who we are. Overall, it tries to remove gender and talk about who we are more in terms of energy, or connecting to the natural world, and metaphors, and meanings, and connections, and signs between ourselves and nature—the animal kingdom or the natural world. We find this

Chapter 4 – The Nest

throughout time and history, and thousands of texts from all over the world connecting us to the same lessons or stories.

The Knowings Method takes us through the seven stages—the seven principles from fear to love that move us back to a place closer to our intuition, closer to love. Each one of the principles is represented by an archetype of a bird.

Fear is represented by the Caged Bird.
Pride is represented by the Peacock.
Courage is represented by the Raven.
Knowings is represented by the Owl.
Forgiveness is represented by the Swan.
Grace is represented by the White Dove.
Love is represented by the Eagle.

When learning the Knowings Method, it is important to understand that there are different feelings and emotions at each level, and that when we become aware of that principle, we can understand how to get to the next level or learn the next principle. But this is not about moving through the levels and just completing something. In fact, that won't work whatsoever.

Knowings is about learning each stage, becoming aware of each stage, and accepting that we are all of the stages and that these spiritual principles are what guide our life and unite us. When we become aware of this, we become aware of the nest. We can be all or one of the stages with every breath we take.

The Nest is the sacred place we go to reflect, and heal, and meditate, and discern, and pray, and listen. When we become aware of the Nest, we can become aware of which one of the principles we need to retreat with and work on in that moment.

The point of learning the Knowings program and understanding the flow of the method is understanding that we can take our healing into our own hands and create a sacred, safe space for it.

At the core of everything is the Nest, the Knowing. This is the God and all-knowing universal source energy, the vibration at the centre of love and fear. This is where you see the signs. This is where you get the owl's eye view because the Knowing is the inner owl, then it expands into rays of love, fear, forgiveness, courage, pride, and fear; they're all connected. They all root back in the Nest.

Birds of the 7 Intuitive Principles

I started spending a lot of time on my own after my separation. I was living on my own, and thanks to a pandemic, the powers of the world decided we should shut down for a few months at a time, on and off for two years. My house backs onto a forest, so I would escape to my Nest in the Crowsnest Pass.

In the Pass, Suzie (who owns the coffee shop and fly fish shop, and also happens to be my fishing guide, Al's, partner) and Dawn (who owns the BnB) are like wisdom women to me. They take care of me down there as I rest as a weary traveler.

They open their Nests to me.

Over those few years, I spent a lot of time driving rural roads.

It's all I could do, alone.

I needed out of my own home that becomes a cage if I stay inside too long, talking to myself or telling Netflix I am still watching.

I started noticing things, different things.

I started noticing birds.

And I started referring back to them and what others told me they meant, and what I felt they meant.

When my grandpa passed, he wanted "On Eagle's Wings" played at his funeral. I can't listen to it without crying. I imagine him soaring with God up there in heaven. It represented something to him that was strong and mighty and intentional. It knew what it was doing, it knew what it needed to do. It represents strength and greatness, something we would want to fly into the afterlife with.

These birds started to come to me after my grandpa died. I started noticing more eagles that reminded me of him, and some herons—birds he loved too. The more I noticed, the more they

Chapter 4 – The Nest

spoke to me. The birds for this model started revealing themselves to me slowly over time. I would see a sign or notice something that lead me to a clue to describe or move closer to what's next.

The caged bird is from my own words in my journals. Whenever I was caged, I was in a self-imposed prison. I put myself there. I acted as if I was there, locked in, when I was the holder of the key. The association is to fear and force, a place the mind cowers under repeating or spinning thoughts.

The Peacock is represented by the male and the female. The association is to pride and ego, which has two sides. We will always have pride and ego—it's our job to have a healthy balance of them, and not have any part of it be on colourful display at all times. When we are acting out in our pride or leading with our ego, trying to force our ways on others, it's as obnoxious as a Peacock squawk, like walking into a wall of feathers that cannot be passed without getting nipped. It's more of a loud boisterous presence—an annoyance. There are two sides to pride and ego though—the more showboating side of posturing and squawking, and the other meeker, more life-giving side. The live-giving side, the female, is usually behind the scenes quietly. The life-giving side to pride and ego is also behind the scenes. The secret to balancing it and having a harmonious swing on the pendulum, is to acknowledge that ego is with us, not going anywhere, and we always have two ways to present it. It can be like a wall that stops us, or it can be a curious life-giving experience.

The Raven represents courage, and it's about the courage to shift your perspective. There are many stories associating these birds (like the crow) with a certain kind of darkness. Just due to its appearance, there is a story cast that it is dark, ominous, and mysterious, almost like it's up to something. What we don't know, or have forgotten, is that with these species, there are also white ravens and white crows. They are very rare, and the ones I'm talking about do not have albino genes. They are the same bird, just with different colours.

My point here is that when we see the black bird, we cast a judgement or story about what it's up to. We cast a prejudice.

And my question is, "Do you have the courage to shift your perspective, and see through the eyes of rarity and wonder that there are other things that can challenge us, in a good way?" Like knowing if we saw a white raven, we wouldn't say that it's here in an eerie place, or that it's up to something. We wouldn't feel a certain chill of fear wondering if it's bringing us an omen.

Courage is about seeing things from another perspective.

The Owl is for Knowing the inner place of quietude and wisdom. When I started tracking Owls and trying to find them, the days I was chasing or trying to force it, I didn't see any. When I went for a walk and trusted that my inner compass was guiding me to where I needed to go, I found them. Yet I had a noticing, a pattern I saw. Every single Owl I saw was looking at me first. When I noticed it, it was already watching me. Some moved their heads in a way that was curious and confused almost, like 'What took you so long?' The Owl and the Nest are the same place, that heart centre within. That inner voice, or inner place is calling you. It sees you first. You need to show up on the path and head in that direction to listen differently.

The Swan is for forgiveness. To forgive is two parts; one is to acknowledge the pain, and the second is to surrender it and let it go. The surrender part we can do, but surrendering is a co-creation. It's a giving and receiving, a reciprocity of sorts. See, a true complete heart made by two swans coming together is about partnership. That's true and complete forgiveness—part of us coming to the table and offering what happened, and the other part is giving it to something else, that source energy, to take away and deal with it. The two parts also represent the logic side and the intuition side. The logic side wants to keep it, fight with it, win with it, revenge with it, and hold onto the misery. The intuitive side is coaxing quietly to release the anger, frustration, and the talks you're having in your head, and just let go. There's another way through if you have the courage to see you don't have to hold onto things that hurt you. You can let them go, and hold boundaries for your pond and what gets allowed into it.

The Dove is for grace. Grace is a mysterious thing, and the

Chapter 4 – The Nest

fact that we have white doves for purity and weddings and celebrations and memorials as something we let go to fly into the unknown is like grace. We know we have to let go and rise above anything that would hold us back from flying free. We need to release any ties to things here to free ourselves to be spirit and God-led, allowing us to feel differently than when we were trying to force and control life to happen our way, out of fear. The Dove was documented Egyptian history 5000+ years ago, and similar accounts of gifting or releasing doves can be found in ancient Chinese, Greek, Roman, and European texts.

The Eagle revealed to me that it represented love. One day travelling home from the Pass, reflecting on the Nest and theories tying birds to each one, an Eagle flew alongside my passenger window. As I was driving, I saw it flying, almost as though it wanted me to get my attention. I pulled over and started my camera. It started to fly in a circle around the field it landed on, and the higher it got, the wider the spiral it created got. It flew and flew, higher and higher, towards the clouds and the sun. After six minutes, I lost sight of it in the sun, as it disappeared into illuminated brilliance. It was shining, like love. It was curious to me too—why did it fly so high where there's nowhere to perch, nothing to eat, and nowhere to go? Why did it keep gaining momentum to go higher? Did it go as high as it could go?

Love is like that when it's truly felt. It's expansive and elusive. Not just love in romantic relationships, but the essence of the great power of love. The essence of the feeling that is higher than any other, just because. The essence that disappears and will reappear another time with a Knowing of why it did what it did.

We can connect our emotional states to the birds, too. Eagles have exceptional self-control and peace. They are very intentional and strategic. Grace is about kindness and gentleness to yourself, and forgiveness is about learning patience in the process of surrender and letting go. Some of these things are elusive, like the Doves flying away quickly or the Swans floating slowly, but they are there.

When we feel like we are in a place we trust, co-create (with spirit or God or others), and can be free, and we are safe and rested and informed in the Nest, we can listen differently to what our next steps are to be. We can express ourselves using words that align with how we see ourselves, from a higher perspective. We can embody those higher vibration terms that we don't feel quite like we are in yet, and we can lean into that and try it on for a while. We feel illuminated, like the golden tree, and we are lighting the way for ourselves and others who come to our light. We are feeling connected to God or a source energy, like we are on the right path, noticing signs and clues to guide us to what's next.

Words you can use when you're experiencing life from a higher perspective and illumination:

- Guided by a source energy (too powerful to be named)
  - Knowing that source energy is available to anyone and everyone if they choose
  - People call it God, Creator, gods, universe, stars, ethers
- Illuminated, brilliance, natural leadership, feels good but can't explain it
- Love, peace, joy, kindness, gentleness, goodness, faithfulness, patience, self-control
- Bliss, enlightened, on the path, in flow
- Surrender - Knowing that the way is to trust and do prayer and meditation
- Signs & Noticing - Knowing that we must listen differently to markers on our way

When we are feeling stuck in our lives, and we are resting in the ease of what's easy because we are too lazy to work towards anything else, we are stagnant. This laziness could come from many things, but what I often find with clients is it comes from a place of complacency, feeling like giving up for no reason, or because it's hard.

Chapter 4 – The Nest

It's supposed to be hard.
It is hard.
And it will be hard again.

The pivot point of those who have the courage to push through that place of uncertainty, and not Knowing, and into a place of Knowing, is courage. The pivot point is in a choice and a decision, one breath. One chance to shift your perspective and life path, or not.

When we choose to stay stuck, we stay in a place that is beneath our skills and abilities, a place where our confidence is shot, and we question our every thought and move and stay paralyzed in fear of making any decision—we choose to keep a mask on and fake life. We don't thrive, we don't grow, and we stay in spin cycles that make us feel sick, like we are digging a bigger hole every day.

So, we put ourselves in the cage and we numb it out. We cope. We drown ourselves in alcohol, or numb out with drugs or gambling. We overstimulate with cheap versions of the real thing with food and sex and feel unsatisfied every time the binge or secret hook-up is over. Then we spin in fear on getting caught, getting honest, feeling the real source of the pain, or overdoing it in some way that hurts other people more than it's hurting us. We act like victims, like it's happening to us, and we seek pity and make up stories to cover up the fact that we are capable of more. We choose to keep feeding the dark side and its evil plans to attach to our minds with obsessions and addictions and lust. We act from a place of fear, often getting our Peacock feathers up and reminding people not to pass. We speak highly of ourselves from a place of pride and ego, masking the pain under the surface of not being good enough, smart enough, attractive enough, etc. And we stay there, behind the bars in our own isolation, withdrawing from the world, while over and over again we have the opportunity to change something, see life from a higher perspective, and let go of what's no longer serving us.

Words you can use when you're experiencing life from a stagnant perspective (cage & spinning).

- Spinning, caged, feathers are up, unwilling to see things differently
- Self-guided, won't let any other insights or perspectives or opinions in
- Self-sabotage, self-harm, abusing self, harmful self-talk, resentful
- Pride, ego, shadow self, dark night of the soul, evil, dark side
- Anxious, angst, angry, inner battles, inner fights, isolate, withdraw
- Blame, regret, revenge, hate, retaliation, humiliation, shame
- Acting out, coping with drugs/alcohol/obsessions, secrets, double-life
- Fuck-its, numb-out, separate from heart, catastrophes in the mind
- The Mask – defend the logic of why, block the feeling of Knowing you need to change

It's fascinating to me that feelings of anxiety and fear are also about withdrawal. They typically come with a sense of grief and regret and getting out of places where you're so ashamed and humiliated, and you blame other people, and feel a sense of guilt and heaviness. The lower vibration is a heaviness and it's that caged feeling.

There's a heaviness to being caged—caged is usually not by choice, but something has its grasp over us with the door closed until we decide to ask, "How do I get out of here?"

However, we can only hear what we are to do when we get to the Nest.

You can go to the Nest, but you don't stay there—we just tune in to know it's there. You get to align it with whatever belief system, or club, or group you ascribe to. It's different for

Chapter 4 – The Nest

everybody, but to be optimistic and willing to see that all of us here—while our belief systems are all different—can get to a higher vibrational place that works for each of us.

Thus, we can move each other to a higher vibrational place just by being together. Because we understand that there are more meaningful experiences out there for us that we didn't see before we tuned into that wisdom. But in our wisdom, we start to attract better, and when we start to attract better, we start to do better. We start to do different things because we don't feel stuck anymore.

We move to a place where maybe we understand that we lacked a sense of discipline or understanding or connection to what we were doing before. We realize we were doing it out of fear and not a place of "Love, joy, peace, patience, kindness, goodness, faithfulness, gentleness, and self-control." [1]

So, when we're applying this in our lives personally, our lives professionally start to shift as well. That is why the OwlSeek applies to leadership as well once we get to a place of Knowing.

Being in the Nest, we then see that there's a greater path ahead.

The path ahead is to come to a place of transcendence.

We accept that there's another way forward. We accept that we don't have to hold on to a previous thought pattern, such as a negative dark thought pattern that wasn't serving us. Maybe it connects with the language you use (e.g., 'ball and chain' or being tied to something in the metaphysical world).

We can see the old way for what it was, or what it is.

Its cords detach and we let it go.

You surrender and let it go and you hope, you pray, and you understand that something else is out there for you, and it will be revealed to you when it's time, and when you're in the state of manifesting versus in the state of forcing.

---

[1] Paul to Galatian (5: 22-23) Fruit of the Spirit.

Manifesting in the Nest

As I mentioned, I have a Great Horned Owl picture in my kitchen from a photographer in the Okotoks area. I imagined him to be some kind of old farmer who also likes to bird-watch. I really love his handmade frames. They're rustic and wooden with rounded corners, and his pictures of birds, while simple, are very clear and have sharp meaning for me. I put the Great Horned Owl picture in my kitchen before I actually saw one in the wild. I had seen some in sanctuaries or at the zoo, but it's not the same as attracting something in the wild.

My first practice with retreating to the Nest to manifest seeing something in the wild was with grizzly bears, and then black bears. I would imagine seeing them, and then they would appear to me. And it was never irrational, and never harmful. It was never anything I cast off as dark energy. It was being in the flow to magnetize and attract what I put in my mind first. I do this with animals because I think it's a safe reciprocal exchange with mother nature. I think if I'm a good conservationist and steward of the land, I will be shown the gifts of the land (but it humiliates my sons when I go around picking up garbage).

I root this practice in some of the wanderers and pioneers before me, so to speak, who spent time out walking the trails, and taking notes, and keeping handwritten journals of all of the animals and insects, and plants and mountain ranges, and water pathways that they saw—just like Kya did in *Where the Crawdads Sing* (2018). I find this kind of mapping and tracking fascinating. And I believe that we can do it in our own mind with our own thoughts, and reconfigure the trails back to where we are called to go. I believe some of this observation and looking from the Nest is us being able to see the trails or pathways we put forth, and when we get that 30,000-foot or 50,000-foot view of our life, we can see that there's actually another way. To see it head on. To see it spiral upward. To see the expansive growth.

But we can't do this without spending time testing what we thought to be true. I find that, often, the greatest disconnection is people trying to force what's not true on to what they want to

Chapter 4 – The Nest

be true. We have to unlearn to learn. It's a process, and requires some intention to have a good look at what parts of yourself you're willing to surrender.

What are you willing to let go of, so you can welcome in what's next for you?

I was taught that there's a big difference between the law of attraction and manifestation. People have the ability to force their will, or their way, on the law of attraction to move them forward a little bit faster. Law of attraction is about declaring, and putting your attention on something, and finding a logical way to make it yours.

Manifesting is about co-creating and surrendering what you're asking from the universe, and letting God do the work. You keep strong in your prayer, and your ask, and carve out time for meditation, listening, and hearing what you're supposed to do or clues to follow. Watching for signs and noticing things on the path are big parts of manifesting. As nature has patterns in the forest, life can create patterns for us to see when we turn our attention towards something else, and are open to welcoming in another way.

Manifesting happens when we let go and have the courage to say, "I want this, but I don't know how it's going to come to me." Manifesting is when we put little symbols and objects around us and we say, "Show me more on your time," to the God, the Universe, the Creator, and the energy that is that source of light for all of us, and that source of breath for us. "Show me. Show me more about this, I'm curious. I'm here as a student. I want to talk to others and teach others what I'm finding, but I also want to learn."

So, when I bought this picture frame with the Owl and I wanted to manifest seeing one in the wild, I knew I needed to manifest it in my mind first. A phrase I'd been reflecting on— "faith without works is dead"—reminded me that if I had the belief that I could see it, I needed to go back and do the work, the research, and the inquiry into 'the how' that Ms. Baxter taught me. I have to show up halfway when it comes to manifesting. So,

I started seeing it in my kitchen first. I started researching where it appears in the wild, and where it appears in the summer versus the spring, fall, and winter. And then, I told a friend.

I told this friend that I wanted to see an Owl in the wild, and he laughed at me a little bit, but also knew the power and intention of my mind. We went on a road trip together to a colony a couple hours away to get some handmade products and some organic food. And on the way back, we got lost. I had said that we were going to see this Owl together. Low and behold, I was the passenger while we were driving and had my eyes glued to the window in a cold, freezing rain. The kind of wind that whips your face and feels like it's slapping you; it was that kind of day. Then I saw the tail feathers of an Owl sticking out on a property. I asked my friend to reverse because I thought I saw it, but didn't know for sure. He gave me a 'Yeah right, Jill,' look and we backed up. And as soon as he saw it, he said, "Holy shit, you did it."

When we got to the property, there were two Owls. It was an old, abandoned property and I still can't figure out what happened on this property. The foundation of a house is left, but everything else is gone. You walk up the three front steps to where the front door would have been and the metal railing is still there, and then it drops into a fifteen-foot hole in the ground. There was garbage strewn around and empties. But there are also active honeycombs planted so I knew somebody was there, possibly the colonies. There were also Quonsets and broken-down vehicles on the property, and I felt like we were being watched by someone else, not just the owls, so I was careful.

All I wanted was a photograph and to connect with the Owls in the wild, and I'm not sure why they called me to this place that I can't get to unless I go to the pin and my GPS, and I literally drive into the middle of nowhere, heading east into the prairies of Alberta, down two hours of dirt roads with hundreds of windmills—windfarms no longer producing agriculture, but creating energy.

I've gone back to visit these owls a couple time, and one of them is a grey Great Horned, and another one is a juvenile white

Chapter 4 – The Nest

Great Horned, and they seem to live together. The older Owl had something happen to one of its eyes. I've gotten close enough with my photos to see that it's recovered, but just doesn't look right. Only one of its eyes is that piercing, yellow colour. He looks older, like he's been there a while, and they live in one of the old barns on the property. I saw them in the window just like I saw in magazines, before I saw them in real life, sitting and looking out.

When I peeked my head in the barn, was the first time I saw an Owl fly towards me with their feet out front. It must have seen or known I was coming first. And I observed the intention of his eyes and the force of his claws, and what it could take from me if it was to actually get a hold of me. It wanted out of the door as fast as I wanted in, and we scared each other, so I left its environment before it came out. I felt like I was trespassing on it. Still, it's one of the most miraculous things I've ever seen. Learning about a species in its environment—when the species is watching you before you see it—is just fascinating.

Retreat
Even as a child, I was attracted to nature. The very first picture that was turned into a painting of me is from when I was about four or five years old. I'm hand-feeding a worm to a little robin in this tiny corner at the property we lived on. Our house in New Dundee, Ontario, had a fence of bushes around it. I found the bushes so comforting to retreat to, as they were like a wall between the sidewalk on the other side, and our property. I loved to go down there and camp out. I'd watch people come and go for their shift work at the creamery across the street. That feeling is still one of my favourites! I can honestly say that, for about a decade, I didn't tune in to how important it was for me to go back to that place.

This place is not only a place of peace and calm and letting my imagination run wild. It's a place of being able to attract things that are of this other world. Being able to be so peaceful and calm that a bird is attracted to you is a thing. Now, I've also had other experiences as a child, like being attacked or shat on by seagulls, and that's a different kind of attraction because the pendulum always has the potential to swing in either direction.

There is a painting in my room to help me remember my inner child, and how innocent and curious she was, and how every day when I wake up, I want to see it and embody that spirit in what I do. I also want to be cautious and cared for, in a sense, as I go through the world as a woman in my 40s. The only way I can do that is to tune into a higher power. That's where I find the arms of spirits so intense, and if we can tune into it, they will wrap around us and keep us safe.

When I'm wandering out in the forest now, there are all kinds of things I fear—like a group of grizzly bears walking out, as that's been something I've experienced. It's something that is so profound that I find people who come to their retreats are able to tune back in, because somehow, we lose it. Somehow, when we stay under the spiritual ceiling of the world, we aren't able to get our energy, our intuition, and our vibration to a place that attracts things like this.

In some cases, people get to a place where they actually repel it, and if something comes near, they're in a constant state of swatting it away, or kicking it. These are people who abuse animals because they can't talk or fight back; it's having lost our self-control in our rage. That's the other side of the pendulum of this little girl in this photo.

The inner rage is a place that means we are so far from the place of inner calm. Now, I can say with all honesty, this is not something we master or that we pray away or lose. We will always have both, and it's up to our self control and practice to calm the rage and manage to live with it. This is something we learn to accept, manage, and live with. This place of inner rage will rise and that's why the Knowings Method is circular, and cyclical, and fluid. We can test it, apply it, adjust it, and repeat it. Because we go into the Nest, we know what skills and tools to grab, and we know what to do. Then we go out into the world and we

Chapter 4 – The Nest

approach it. We constantly need to remind ourselves of what's in that Nest. If we are blocked at one of the seven points, we can dive deeper into why we are in fear, or lacking courage, or unable to let go, or choosing lust over love, and so on.

What's in that safe corner of the bushes where we can retreat? What is that wisdom that we can gather there? Where is that light that we can get our energy source from? What kinds of things can we observe in nature of how they're getting through challenges, and challenging times, and how we can too? What kind of noticings and discoveries can we have with the approach to something so innocent? Like a child and a little bird, how can we approach other things that might teach us deeper lessons about our relationships, our societies, and our work?

While we can go away to nature or a far-off land to retreat, we can also retreat on the metaphysical level where people claim, like monks to an ashram, they can go in their mind. This is where people do a 40-day vision quest, or 40 days of going into the wilderness, going into retreat, and going into self.

However, some can also take this too far. I saw a woman in the days that followed Christmas this year. Her daughter called for an emergency appointment. She was heartbroken. In the days before Christmas, her son, who was in his 20s, went to sleep on the couch and didn't wake up. No drugs, no alcohol, but something was wrong with his heart and he chose not to seek help. She wept, telling me the last thing she said to him was, 'I don't want anything to happen to you' and she went to bed. And then it happened. A year ago, her husband also passed of something heart-related. She was deep in grief, and deep in loss.

Her faith had moved to YouTube teachings of self-proclaimed professors talking about the 2D, 3D, and 5D worlds. How we are part of expansive programs and system and so on. She was in the clouds, rooted in nothing. Her life for fifteen years was raising her three children with her travelling pastor husband who had her living an entirely differently belief system, including doctrines of telling in Baptist communities in the southern states. These are some of the worst kinds of man-made rules and ways to conform—ways that go totally against the grain of the natural state of what we know, versus what we're told.

She hadn't been listening for a long time. I counselled her on my couch in my home as she wept, and we brought the pendulum back to middle instead of hooked on the far sides of telling and curiosity. Somewhere, we have to land in something. Somewhere, we have to root. Somewhere we have to decide that a new set of thoughts, beliefs, and actions are true. A new Nest.

Her daughter texted me the next day and said there was a transformational change in her mom after seeing me. They made it to the funeral home after seeing me to plan their second family funeral in a year. Now it's up to her to keep her pendulum swinging, know that inner Nest place, and breathe into possibility of a new life.

The Nest is where there's retreat, and this is where people go quiet. The mystics before us retreated to the wilderness, sat quietly, lived modestly, and devoted their lives to a source. They believed and had faith it would provide for them. Some did it in ritual and tradition, others did it on their own, following their visions. They'd go find that connection between what they're told, and what they believe about God.

Three Deep Breaths
There's a secret to getting into the Nest—and it's through your breath. That's right, *your breath*. To access the door differently, you have to calm your central nervous system and shift your listening.

For most people, this can be done with three deep breaths.

The first breath grounds you, gets you balanced, brings the pendulum back to centre.

The second breath releases the stress you're carrying that is not yours. Releases what is added to your shoulders and your plate and your thoughts as expectations by others.

The third breath tunes you into you, your central nervous system comes down, and your breathing slows. Since there's been a large exhale, you can rest into you.

Chapter 4 – The Nest

You're now ready to listen differently. Who's with you in the Nest? Who is the Knowing?

Some say God, or god, or gods, or Source, or Allah, or Yawye, or the great I AM, and for many, it's the Universe. For the sake of this book, choose the term that works for you.

In this method, no one name is greater than any another. Although one energy is greater.

We all have access, we all have opportunity, and we all have the right.

We all have the choice—this or that?

In fact, I align more with what Lao Tzu said—if you can name it, that's not it.

The name that can be named is not the eternal name. - Lao Tzu

If you can name it, it's too small, too weak, and it's just a concept.

The real thing, the real God / Creator / Universe or whatever you wish to call it, cannot be named. It can only be felt.

The OwlSeek Method is about diving into your own life and doing some analytical journaling around it, and testing your theories on yourself, your values, your mindset, and your essence. And then feeling into it.

Carl Jung, a Swiss psychiatrist and the father of Analytical Psychology, developed a theory on the collective unconscious. He studied his own journals from 1914–1930 and created ways to measure what he was experiencing.

Knowing your own darkness is the best method for dealing with the darkness of other people. To quote Jung, 'One does not become enlightened by imagining figures of light, but by making the darkness conscious. The most terrifying thing is to accept oneself completely. Your visions will become clear only when you can look into your own heart. Who looks outside, dreams; who looks inside, awakes.'

OwlSeek is data for your soul, an analytical look at your choices and beliefs to see if what you're doing is aligning with who you're called to be. It's a look at where that is coming from (likely an unconscious state or a story you have attached onto to make true).

OwlSeek is your way, aligned and connected to a higher power or source energy. The practice of Carl Jung's methods of analysis are just as important as the practice of connecting with this source of information on moving forward, not just staying in observation. You can find the data of your soul and see where your growth is, and where your stagnancy is, and map out how to turn desire into plans.

I believe many get lost in the conformity of organized religions, which promise salvation in their own ways. There are thousands of ways of a path to the same place that Jung and many mystics before him talked about. People get lost when they follow man-made, man-led movements and doctrines. It's lost in the direct deposit membership—like God on auto-ship—and we're too shameful to cancel the delivery.

People lose connection with themselves and connection to their souls when they move away from who they really are, and get lost or stuck, and give their power to the belief or energy of someone or something else. People also get lost in the wearing of the masks, trying to hide who they really are for the sake of being like everyone else. Not wanting to ruffle feathers, not wanting to be too much of themselves, especially when it goes against the grain of what everyone else is doing to just fit in. We get weak and dependent on things we are trying to force that don't fit. Things that others say to do, or books, or classes following gurus, or buildings like temples and churches.

The greatest gift is in the understanding of the Knowings model and the OwlSeek Method and applying them to your own life once you've removed your unconscious biases and prejudices, and honestly reflect on what's not working. Only then can the door swing open into another way, the lighter way, where we are more alike than we are different.

There's no destination with this model. There's only an understanding of a basic principle that the only constant is change.

Chapter 4 – The Nest

The Knowings is about breathing into the now, the present, and feeling where you're at.

Knowings is:
Love
Grace
Forgiveness
Knowing
Courage
Pride
Fear

Knowing - Who you are	OwlSeek - What you do	Bird - Representative Image
Love *I am*	Leadership *Power + Brilliance*	Eagle
Grace *I feel*	Transformation *Change + Different*	Dove
Forgiveness *I change*	Co-Create *Connection + Evolution*	Swan
Knowing - Intuition *I know - I intuit*	Knowing - Intuition *Values + Trust*	Owl - The Nest
Courage *The Surrender*	Courage *Shift + Surrender*	Raven
Pride *The Ego*	Ego *Projection + Pride*	Peacock
Fear *The Pain*	Control *Force + Fear*	Caged Bird

Chapter 5 – Choices and Change

On April 13, 2006, I was living in Seoul, South Korea, on another geographical cure runaway. I'd graduated from University of Calgary by this point.

When I was in University, I was using cocaine six days a week and working at a rundown pub in Motel Village. There were traffickers that would sit by the windows of this hexagon club looking out over a two-storey motel. I would observe them coming into the pub, giving the pimps money, and then being told what room to go to.

They knew I knew.

They'd slip me flaps of cocaine to keep me quiet.

For years, I lived this double life at university while I studied International Development and African Studies. I'd been to Ghana on a field school. I'd been to Nigeria. I'd been to Egypt. I'd been to France and Costa Rica.

I was studying human trafficking all over the world.

And here I was participating in it in Calgary.

One day a woman came out on a gurney, and that was the big change for me—the realization that somebody had died. With that, I decided something needed to change, so I tried treatment a few times.

I ran away to South Korea to get away from that life because I wanted to go to a place where drugs were illegal. I got an amazing job teaching English and they paid for my flight and my room. I was hired for my appearance. I was placed on teacher assignment in a prep school. I was told how to dress, that I should get laser treatments to make my skin creamier, lose 30 lbs, and wear more makeup. None of it was healthy for my body image.

But what I didn't know was how to only drink because I'd been drinking with cocaine for years. I also didn't know how independent and powerful I thought I was, when I'd given everything away.

One Friday night I went out by myself, and I didn't come home.

The bar was down in the Itaewon District, which is like their Vegas—it's this melting pot of teachers, military, expats, and diplomats.

I met these guys in the bar.

I got drinks from them and then I started to feel really weak. I started to feel like I was on GHB, which is the date rape drug we used to take in smaller doses for fun in Calgary as a party drug, so I knew what it felt like.

I left the club, and I went outside to the alley.

I needed some air.

I was going to try to get a taxi, but then I started to fade. I leaned on the brick wall. All I could smell was food from night carts in the alley—fried food, rice cakes, red pepper sauce—a sour smell. *I need to just sit down and sleep here.* And then a car pulled around the corner and it was the guy from the bar.

The last thing I remember was him grabbing me by my shoulders, and laying me down in the backseat of the car. He lifted my legs into the car. I could see it all happening but I couldn't move, and then the door closed, and then I don't remember.

When I woke up, I was in an apartment, bound to a chair. I opened my eyes to see a video camera across the room and bloody, beady eyes. I heard two male voices. *I'm naked. There's all this stuff around me, and he's sitting beside me.*

Suddenly, something Ms. Baxter told me came to mind. 'We're not powerless, but we give our power away.' I had written it down in my journals. It's also the first step in recovery programs that says we are powerless, and our lives had become unmanageable.

It all started to connect.

Chapter 5 – Choices and Change 69

I had given my power away, thinking I was so independent and could always get myself home. And this time I couldn't.

He held me for two days. He got tired of me. I was too loose to be raped again. All he had left was humiliating and physically beating me.

I found what clothes I could, and I left.

I didn't have money. I didn't have my wallet. I didn't have my phone. I ran outside and a taxi driver picked me up by some grace of God. I called him an earth Angel. We couldn't speak to each other. I didn't know what region I was in. I couldn't read the signs. I couldn't tell him my address. I was a mess.

Because of how I looked and because we were close to the American military base, he thought that I must be American, so he just dropped me off at the guard house on base.

Two soldiers helped me in. They started asking questions and I think they put it together before I did. I was trying to not tell anybody, to make this disappear.

I didn't want this to be something.

I ended up signing over that they would deal with it. What I now know is this happened off base. This happened with somebody from the base. This happened on Korean soil so it would have to be a Korean investigation.

I didn't want anyone to know.

My plan was to take it to the grave.

I thought I'll just get better.

They gave me a checkup. They gave me a social worker and told me about a recovery program that met weekly on the base, and that's where I started going to meetings. Then, they got me home.

I've never drank since.

The Fuck-its

Reading through my journals, I found that I would often tell myself that I didn't know what to do, and I would sit and spin in anxiety and fear.

I would freeze or I would run.

I would escape to different workshops or conferences.

I would escape to different weekends away with friends and hope that I would find something in those places outside myself that would reveal to me what I was to do.

The longer I was looking outside for these things, the more I felt like I was forcing myself into my own illusionary cage. When opportunities came for me to open the door and fly away, I would shut down and sit in the self satisfaction of the fuck-its.

The fuck-its are a state where you know you're doing something wrong, and you choose to do it anyway. The fuck-its are a state where you know you should say 'no' but you say 'yes,' where you don't care if you disappoint or harm other people with vindictive and vengeful behaviour that you blame on other people, places, and things. Blame is another fuck-it, too.

These states are where we identify what pride is and how it plays a role in either keeping the mask on, keeping the illusion alive, or taking it off and being able to see what it is and what a tragedy it would be to hide behind it.

Instead, we have the courage to choose to change—to step out of that place where we feel bound by a ball and chain. We must acknowledge that we're scared and frightened to have the courage to move to the next level. But we know that we don't want to be in this place anymore, that we're living with aggressive words and actions directed at ourselves and other people. Instead, we believe it's possible and feasible to get to a new place. We accept that we can change things—by making a decision.

When we come from the place of pain (which is our fear) and we try to keep covering it with the mask (which is our ego) we're not surrendering, and we can stay stuck in the bottom loop projecting all of our blame and anger and hatred on others and forcing the cycle to continue until we either get sick, or others cannot tolerate us anymore. And we find ourselves more and more isolated or withdrawn. Or we find ourselves hanging out with people in places we shouldn't be, keeping us stuck in secrets, living a lie, and showing up masked.

Chapter 5 – Choices and Change

We can become indifferent to how our actions actually affect other people. No one likes someone who is indifferent, that they cannot trust or don't value their participation.

All of this shifts in the middle, in the Nest, at the Knowings phase, where we start to not only believe with our logical mind that we need to change, but our body is physically telling us we need to change.

Or we just feel something inside. And we don't know how we're hearing it or sensing it or feeling it or knowing it. But we do hear the call from within, and we trust it. Like when my dad hurt me in a blackout—doing things no one should do especially to a daughter—I wept as I held my infant son vowing to protect him from the same pain while still battling the addiction that should never have touched me.

This is the stage that I call 'the spiritual two-hand shove.' Sometimes when we are stuck in a pattern, or a loop, or a process because we're trying to control and force the outcome, we're creating so much tension between natural flow and ourselves that the universal God has to step in and give us a spiritual two-hand shove to knock us down, just so we can pull ourselves back up.

Sometimes this is physically felt like 'I'm getting a nudge from the other side'—like when I felt Chuck's embrace, looking over my shoulder to see if there was something there. Usually this is telling me to leave and let go of whatever I'm trying to force or hold onto, like hanging on to a metal pipe until our fingers just give out and we fall.

But sometimes the fall is exactly what we need to do over and over and over. We teach this to toddlers from infancy, and the greatest lessons for them are learning how to pick themselves up and move forward.

My friend Jen has been through the fall of the spiritual two-hand shove a few times. After moving down to California to complete her master's and teach at a forward-thinking tech high school, she had to experience immense loss when her time there was cut short. After a bad bicycle accident that landed her in the hospital, and having her parents fly down to bring her back to the Canadian health care system, she crashed again when she got better. Everything she thought she was building and doing was taken away from her. Everything she thought she was working towards and the people and partnerships she imagined having were gone, never to return.

Having to sit in healing, rehabilitate her brain and legs and body, and take time away from working and studying and building her career had her depressed, sad, and uncertain of what was ahead. She took work teaching at other programs when she came back to the city she chose to live in, but nothing was lighting her up.

You see, she was doing work that she could always do.

But who she was? She wasn't so sure of that.

And when she reflected, who she was in California wasn't who she wanted to be either. It was more of a chase. But to what end?

After some time off, and then landing other contract work that was similar to her work in California, the universe stepped in again with another two-hand shove.

This time she was riding an e-scooter as she thought it was safer than getting on another bike again. Low and behold, there was a malfunction in the locking mechanism and when she went over some uneven terrain from roots growing through concrete, she landed on her face again, only this time the scooter collapsed, crushing her ankle. It's now held together with titanium rods and synthetic parts.

And what did she have to sit and think about?

A lot.

A lot of wonder of how you can move geographical locations and have the same experience repeat itself. Wondering what lesson she met the first time. Wondering what she needed to do this time to finally learn what she was supposed to learn.

In her healing, she had a lot of time to think about that. Again, the work suffered and she had to reflect on what she was doing. She could always go back to work she had already done, applying skills she had applied before, again. But why? And what

Chapter 5 – Choices and Change

did she need to learn about making meaningful changes that were not going to produce the same kind of patterns, again? Now she's balancing her mental health, working with professionals to find the right doses to keep her balanced and well, including eating healthy and staying hydrated, and able to see and bring joy into her life.

Jen has come for one-on-one counsel and weekend-long retreats, done the 8-week digital course, and she's still on the walk. She's constantly diving into the stories she told herself are true, and uncovering the lies that had a hold on her.

To see what's next for herself, she's doing something different now.

She's listening differently. She's listening within. She's asking the hard questions.

She's saying 'no' to contracts that come up that are similar to those that came before, because now that she has been able to analyze some of the data of her soul, she's able to see that just because she's capable of doing something, doesn't mean it aligns with who she is ultimately called to be. In this period of life as she navigates the 'what's next' as a single woman in her 40s with no relationship and no kids, she wonders what all that work was for anyways. Now she's making decisions that align with her values, stepping into what she does, and planning a life ahead that brings a lot of groundedness, slowing down, and noticing the signs on the pathways through life.

When I met Luke, I could tell he was between two worlds. The tattoos and steroid-induced muscles told one story, the mask of the hardness of life, and the sad eyes of a man who just wanted to feel like he knew he was on the right track and moving somewhere good told another story. The truth was, he wasn't moving somewhere good. The steroids he was using for working out were black market, and the people who were hustling those always had the next best scam up their sleeves, too. When we met, the conversation started around what to do with the 'hot' (stolen) motorcycle in his living room, which he was holding for a friend. That friend was the dealer who was holding it as compensation for a deal gone bad, and Luke was just helping his friend.

The energy of that 'helping out' came with more than he asked for.

Every time he came home and would see that bike, he saw the life he was participating in. He knew it wasn't good. He knew that life was a mask from the life he was living with his family— a close family, where the mom of three sons was going through chemo again, for another cancer, after she'd already been through a couple bouts.

When asked about his mom, Luke couldn't talk about it. He didn't have the courage to put words to the sadness he felt to have a mom, the matriarch of all boys, be unwell and unable to live life to the fullest, again.

He was able to master the mask of the tough guy with a tough front and organized crime badge with the kind of societal acceptance he was wanting—a family of sorts. But it turns out, fucked-up families are fucked-up families.

The more he was around this dark life and dark activities, the less he felt like himself and the more he felt like a puppet trying to be like everyone else. The pride and boasting ego of being so tough is like a bird yelling from a cage to be seen, and not knowing why authentic connections are hard, why relationships are hard. See, when we're in this place, we tend to only meet other birds in cages, or people who think they can save or fix the birds in the cages. Neither are healthy or ideal.

And without knowing it, his moral compass was screaming to change course. Find another flight path. Not rooting the moral compass in any one faith or religion or spiritual understanding, Luke displayed the only two things necessary to start listening to where this comes from—curiosity and desire.

He was curious if there was another way. He would often look at me and wonder how I let things go. When I would tell him to let things go, he would wonder 'how?' He desired to feel

Chapter 5 – Choices and Change

differently. On his quest, he listened to me talk about wanting to attract Owls. He went for a massage with a girl he knew, and she did a reiki-like look into him. She told him she sees an Owl in him, and he called and told me after the appointment. He then walked his dog at the dog park and, wouldn't you know, I get a photo of a Great Horned Owl in the middle of the day on branches in the spring where there are no leaves to hide in. In plain sight. Jealous, I expressed how I was happy for him but inside I was burning. I've been manifesting and researching and tracking Owls to see one like this, and now he gets to?! And you know what? Life's like that. It's not fair. And the jealousy was the opportunity for me to see if I use it as ruffling of my feathers, or something more life-giving on my path. I chose the latter.

Over time, Luke settled into his calling for work, and got himself on a healthier track. He's a devout follower of '75Hard,' a mental discipline and fitness plan for hardcore people. The gym is his church, and he's now open and willing to having hard conversations and working on his relationships. He put sound mentors in his life, other entrepreneurs who do freelance and contract work. I've never known the guy to miss a gym day, and he's constantly working on his prized possession (his legs) in a healthy way, whereas most meatheads like him are working on their shoulders. He sees the world a little bit differently now. He sees the pathway as his own, and we need more of that.

We have to surrender this process so that we will observe and learn and listen and hear different things that become our truths. Then we see the choices in front of us and can discern or dissect whether they're coming from a place of fear or love. We also start to feel like we're moving to a higher vibration. Things start to feel more hopeful, and trusting ourselves and our values starts to feel like an inspiring place to be, like there's more harmony with our surroundings.

When we get to this place, we relax the muscles in our face, smile at strangers, offer compliments, hold doors, and leave kind comments online. Suddenly, life starts to feel like it has meaning again, and we feel joy and love in the things we do.

Burnouts, Breakdowns, and Breakthroughs
Two things I know for sure:
1. Burnout causes breakdowns, in our routines, habits, and flow.
2. Breakdowns lead to breakthroughs with a spiritual two-hand shove in another direction.

I have quirks, sometimes things scare me or remind me of things from my past. I swung at my ex-husband when he grabbed my shoulder from behind one time, a nice, normal gesture when dating. However, for me it was a 'trigger' of something I couldn't get away from.

I cannot be confined or tied up for fun. In an instant, I flip and think I can't get out, and panic sets in.

I cannot be around any dark arts or those casting spells to harm others, as my soft soul cannot handle it. It's playing with low vibrations and not going to a high enough source.

I have good quirks too. Things that made me forgive everything and everyone who harmed me.

That took decades of work for me.

I'm more than two decades into my spiritual journey work and more than seventeen years in recovery from an alcohol and cocaine addiction. I am sober from those two things and believe in harm reduction, as cannabis helps me thrive. I've recently heard it called 'California sober.'

Therefore, when we bring this death to the spin cycle and take it to a spiral, that's the death of the logic attachment to the spin. When we retreat, we put to death this idea of living in burnout, and that living in burnout (even though it's going to kill us) means we have to stay in it. We put to death the idea that we can't calm ourselves with breath.

Spiraling up, or spiraling down
Having the courage to surrender is making a decision to change, and identifying the clues and coincidences that will help push us

Chapter 5 – Choices and Change

to a new growth place, a new direction, and create new plans with intentions.

This is where we feel the spiritual two-hand shove.

When we act from a place of ego, over and over, and acting from a place of fear, that is what can stop us. We can continue the cycle, or we can start to tune into feeling differently, creating new archetypes, and creating new visions of who we want to be.

We do this by paying attention to what we're seeing, reading, listening to, watching, hearing, and aligning ourselves with—either more of the path that we were on, or more of the paths that we want to be on—and we have to become willing to see another way.

We also have to identify that these two-hand shoves are sometimes consequences.

Some belief systems call them 'karma,' some call them 'punishments' from a power greater than us—but I don't believe in that for a second. These are too often man-made institutions of Catholic or Mormon control, such as women lying to each other, forced by men to embrace the eternal role of a mother both here and on the other side. This reminds me of the quote from *Women Talking* (2018): "The truth is that she's not crazy. The truth is that she's been driven crazy."

I believe these things are more like course correction and awareness.

Lessons can come to us through consequences (and when things don't go our way) through noticing, gut feelings, dreams, visions, and plans.

There is no bad or wrong place to be in the OwlSeek method. There is no such thing as a 'bad' construct of the mind that would dictate that you are also 'bad.'

If we tie some dark cloud of religious doctrine over our head, with sinning as a consequence, it can feel like you have a duty and an obligation to make it right. The problem with that, as many of those constructs have been man-made, is that people are put under the pressure of other people or belief systems that make them feel like they're in scarcity or lack and can't crawl out of the black cloud of whatever indoctrination they've been led to believe.

The truth is, we're allowed to shift our belief systems.

The truth is, even if we've been raised with religious doctrine that told us something logically, we can know in our body that it's not true.

You have permission and are allowed to explore this, lest we be burned by men and bound by control.

Diving into this needs a map or a guide to answer the right questions along the way, to get to your own destination, and that's what the OwlSeek Method and workbook offers—a way to clear your path. Find out more at www.owlseek.ca/.

We need to shift our perspective and look at these bad things as challenges that we can learn and grow from. We step into the space of acknowledging that we are getting challenges or lessons or assignments or tests (but I don't like the word 'tests' because I don't think we're physically tested by the force of something else on the other side). I think we are more given the opportunity in our freewill to objectively look at things and assess whether we're on our path. So, from the Nest, you can either stay in low vibration, stay in self, and stay in subjective self-saying, or you can see that higher perspective. And when you make your logic self your guiding light, you're too influenced by the lower veil of the world. That lower veil of the world in the diagram has a heavy-headed logic cloud that keeps people stuck.

Some people had parents, or guardians, or teachers, or influences around them that held these low vibrational energies. Some people stay in man-made religions and low vibrational energies, spinning their whole life.

When we step into more of a spiritual maturity place, which is what the Nest offers, we can reflect on what we were taught, and sit, and see if it was true or not.

When people get stuck in a low vibrational state, they go back to the only place they know to try to get out of it—your parents, your advisors, or your mentors in your organized belief system.

Chapter 5 – Choices and Change 79

Or you do something external to distract and escape, like take another workshop, or another class, or you become a little bit of a program jumper where you don't actually follow through on anything you've learned.

Or you have an affair and live a double life.

These things also need to be reflected on, and we can only do that when we detach from everything and holistically look it all over.

We need the courage to ask who's in our corner, and the courage to ask if the people that we've surrounded ourselves with are actually helping to move us forward. Really go higher in the Nest and, with a bird's eye view, see who those people are that we are hanging out with, and what those influences are, because that energy comes back and impacts us.

People are allowed to make decisions, and go back to relationships, and go back into their own cycles and patterns. If you're walking alongside someone and notice a lower vibration while you're trying to go higher, you're going to have to decide whether you're going to walk away, or if you're going stay in it. If you're going stay in it, you have to recognize that you're just returning to the same cycle pattern loop, stuck at a low vibration with this person.

This is a choice.

This choice can be made in work environments, churches, friendships, personal environments, clubs, and associations.

You have the opportunity in every single given moment to look at all of this.

Spiritual two-hand shove
The Universe will move you to where you need to be.

The Universe will show you how inappropriate you are, with whom, and where to go.

The Universe will give you a two-hand shove to move you to where you need to be, and with whom.

We don't know how we're hearing it, or sensing it, or feeling it, or knowing it. But we do hear the call from within, and we can trust it. This is the stage that I call the spiritual two-hand shove. When we are stuck in a pattern, or a loop, or a process because we're trying to control and force the outcome, we're creating so much tension between natural flow and ourselves that the universal God has to step in and give us a spiritual two-hand shove.

Sometimes this is physically felt for me, like I'm getting a nudge from the other side, and I'm looking over my shoulder to see if there's something there. Usually this is telling me to leave and let go of whatever I'm trying to force or hold on to. Sometimes the fall from the metal bar we can't grip anymore is exactly what we need to do over and over and over.

We have to surrender this process so that we can observe, and learn, and listen, and hear different things that become our truths, and we see the choices in front of us and can better discern or dissect whether they're coming from a place of fear or love.

We also start to feel like we're moving toward a higher vibration. Things start to feel more hopeful, trusting ourselves and our values within starts to feel like an inspiring place to be, and there's more harmony with things that are around us. When we get to this place, we relax the muscles in our face and smile at strangers, offer compliments, hold doors, and leave nice comments online. Suddenly, life starts to feel like it has meaning again, and we feel joy and love in the things we're doing. With grace, we feel different, and we're okay to let go of what has to go.

I spent the first decade of my career wanting to make moves, and give people's stories, and be this disrupter and change-maker, and I thought I had to be behind the scenes of everything. And very intentionally, I was, and the result was that I ended up not having control of what I was doing, and when it was time, I felt the spiritual two-hand shove.

You might have heard the call a couple of times to make changes, and pivot, but you may still be saying, "No, no, no—not

Chapter 5 – Choices and Change

yet. Later. It's okay for now to keep going with it. Maybe I'll try it a different way." And what you're hearing is, "Shut it down. Shut it. Down." But that ego attachment doesn't want you to separate from it, even though you know you need to, and so the spiritual two-hand shove comes along and can't be ignored. It's a hockey reference to the crosscheck from behind that you don't see coming.

It wrecks your plans, and then you've got to pick up the pieces.

When my marriage ended, it ended because I told him I couldn't do it anymore. And there was a relationship I didn't know about. It was time for me to leave my home, his house.

At the time I heard, "This will be as hard as you make it." And the second thing I heard was, "If you truly believe in forgiveness, grace, and love, then in one breath you'll exercise that." I believe the spiritual two-hand shove comes in and through us as something that is planted in our mind as a Knowing, or it comes in and through our heart centre where we feel it first.

Chapter 6 – The Shadow

Fear and Control

As I read through my journals of me trying to make it in the work world, I realize how plagued I was by fear and comparison, trying to control and force myself into an environment where I didn't belong, staying despite how I felt on the outside. It's not that people there didn't accept me. It's like I was trying to conform to them, and I didn't like what that represented. So, I didn't like me for trying to be like them.

Then my pendulum would swing too far to the other side and I would hook, forcing myself to try to stay there. Forcing myself to conform.

I recall, as early as fourteen years old, never ever being comfortable in a group of friends. Whether I didn't feel like I had the same Club Monaco sweater, or the same rec club membership, or parents who were 'the same as alllll the others,' I felt like an odd duck as a teenager. I was scared to mix.

But I was courageous. I always listened within, even then, and found signs and clues to help me move closer to where I wanted to be. I felt like other people had parents that helped guide them—choosing schools or sports or after-school activities for them. But I didn't feel like I had that. I never felt connected—not to myself, my parents, my community, my friends—nothing. But I did feel connected when I would talk to myself, and somehow felt an answer come.

A guide. Something I could trust to take me on my way when I didn't think other people were. There was hope. There was comfort. There was light.

This was a different voice than 'the chase.' The chase voice is a whisper of the dark side. The shadow side. The side that makes you feel like you aren't good enough.

The side that makes you fear the pain. It all stems from being stuck on the logic ceiling worldview. You can't imagine a way out, so you just spin here. There's no surrender to pop out of the spin cycle. We have to dive into what information or knowledge we're missing, and have the courage to surrender and say, "I don't know. I don't know what I need. But I know the signs I'm seeing around me are keeping me stuck, or keeping me around low vibration people, or bad energy. I don't leave places feeling filled up—I leave places feeling empty. I am 'dancing with the devil' so to speak, or I am entertaining things that I want to keep a secret in my life."

It's about control, and trying to force the outcome, knowing it's coming from a place of fear. When we dive in and make a list of everything that feels forced and out of control, we have to look at where we are blaming other people or denying our own role, or responsibility, or participation, and see where we're acting from a place of humiliation or shame because maybe that thing is not for us. Having to surrender and let go of that thing (that we thought was the thing for us) is one of the hardest lessons to learn.

Usually, we have to take a look at where we are doing everything we can—and 'doing' is the key word here—to make it seem like we are okay, and status quo, and comparing ourselves to others. With this, we're trying to force our way to where we want to be instead of allowing ourselves to be guided from that internal Knowing place to where we are supposed to be. In the state of fear and control, we see where we want to be from a construct that we lock in with our logic mind as an illusion, and we try to force it. Forcing it over and over and over is acting out of our ego.

When we are in a place of fear, we're trying to control something that can never be controlled. We're living a life that may be miserable, and we despise waking up every single day.

Mask it. Fake it. Fuck it.

Chapter 6 – The Shadow

We are humiliated that we have settled into a path that we thought we should do because everyone else was doing it. It's what society and systems set forth as the only way, when people focus on it all too logically and are not connected to their intuitive self. We turn to coping with things, making us depressed, and anxious, and withdrawn, and numb, forever escaping. We find logic solutions to numb the pain with pharmaceuticals, and never truly feel our way through something. We try to project to the world that we are ok, measuring up just like everyone else. Comparing. Fearing. Doubting. Staying in a stagnant place, churning gossip and blame and criticism for why someone else can do it and we can't.

The Knowings Method is something personal that I had to look at when I was stuck in different phases and feeling like I was stagnant in a low vibe. I felt like I was stuck in a pattern, and a loop, and I was settling in so many areas of my life. Logically, this was a hard argument to understand because, on the outside, my life looked good—it looked like it should look. Married with children in a nice home with a good career.

I would tell myself that I didn't know what to do.

I would sit and spin in anxiety and fear.

I would freeze, or I would run.

I would escape to different workshops or conferences; I would escape to different weekends away with friends, and hope that I would find something in those places outside myself. Something that would reveal to me what I was to do.

The longer I was looking outside for these things, the more I felt like I was forcing myself into my own illusionary cage.

When opportunities came for me to open the door and fly away, I would shut down and sit in the self-satisfaction of the fuck-its—where you know you should say 'no' but you say 'yes.'

These states are where we identify what pride is, and how it plays a role in either keeping the mask on and the illusion alive, or taking it off and being able to see what the mask truly is and what a tragedy it would be to hide behind it.

Instead, we have the courage to step out of that place where we feel bound by a ball and chain, and identify that we're scared and frightened to have the courage to move to the next level. But we do know that we are not wanting to be in this place anymore, that we're living with aggressive words and actions directed to ourselves and other people. Instead, we have to believe it's possible and feasible to get to a new place. And we accept that we can do it.

Making a decision when we come from the place of pain, is our fear, and trying to cover it with the mask, is our ego.

Ego & Pride

We will always have ego. We have the choice to be using pride as something harmful, or applying humility as something helpful. We will always have a kind of shadow self that is the dark to the light. The one shoulder of choice that's not the one on angel wings. The one who dabbles in the dark side. The one who worships self and isn't fueled or filled by any other higher power or source greater than oneself. The fuel that is only looking out for self.

The pendulum swings from the ego-fuelled, prideful, righteous side to the ego-partnered, quiet, humble side. And then there's the middle, where you're confident making a decision, especially when it's a difficult one. When you're ready to choose the other path, the other way, after you've been seeing it for a while. It's a Knowing that there is another way.

One of the hardest things to do is to fold to your own ego—the one you've been holding onto, white-knuckling it and lying to everyone else to wear the mask and show up as you think they want you to show up, until you can't do it anymore.

The next hardest thing is getting honest and standing in your truth. The truth. The truth that is yours coming through you in that moment.

It usually sounds like:
I need to take this mask off.
This isn't me (anymore).

Chapter 6 – The Shadow

I can't keep living this lie.
I don't want to do it like this anymore.
I need a change; this is making me sick from within.
I dislike my life and everything in it when I'm (fill in the blank).

Ego loves to hold onto a story of resentment, too.

It loves to loathe in the stories of things we didn't get, things we lost, ways we were victimized, and ways we were humiliated. Yet, we rewrite the story as though we are the victor, not victim—not in a hero sense, but more in a forced recognition sense. Like a child saying, 'Watch me jump! Watch me! Watch me!' We know that child is screaming for attention, to be seen— normal developmental things.

When we are screaming at ourselves from within, it is not the Owl in the Nest inner voice. It is the caged-bird-that-needs-to-be-in-the-wild squawk.

I was someone who never felt good enough or smart enough. I was a ball and chain to my past darkness that made me feel like there was always an imaginary shadow over myself. No amount of confession, therapy, workshop, or alternative energy clearing was making it better. There's not enough sage in the world to smoke out this block, and the people who put their crystals down me from crown to pelvic zone were not having much success in taking my blocks away either.

It turns out that when you're holding on, demanding to be right, it's blocked.

It turns out that when you like the victim story, it's blocked.

It turns out that when you are wearing it like a badge of honour and not balanced with humility, it's blocked.

Our ego is a state of mind. It's a place that we're consciously aware of, and it's where we choose to do it anyway. We know it's selfish. We know it's coming from a place that is only serving ourselves. And while we know what we are doing, we decide to do it anyway. Even if it's not good for the group, or ourselves.

The group can be our family, our co-workers, our communities, or our friends. At this stage, we have to identify where we're getting prideful, boastful, or arrogant in how we're showing up, and identify our selfishness and define our ego.

Throughout addiction, my journaling was dark. Oftentimes, I would write in the early morning hours when I was in physical body pain, withdrawing from chemicals. I'd write pages and pages of plans, a future arising for myself to not have another night like the night before. There are hundreds of these pages. Often these were alongside plans for changing my body, or eating differently.

Throughout the years of pain, I wanted anything to be true other than the fact that I had an addiction. But the pain and the suffering got so deep, and I was trying to force and control everything around me.

And at some point, when you try to bend metal, it's going to snap.

Writing through the early years of deciding to put down my ego meant I had to surrender to my addiction and have the courage to completely change my life, my friends, and my environment, and shift my way of thinking. That period of surrender and writing had me shift my energy and my vibration to find new things in the world to follow. Things like authors, and theories, and crystal stores, and trending clothing, and body piercing.

At some point I started writing about the nudges that spirit gave me, when it gave me the spiritual two-hand shove to pay attention and notice that there were things in the world around me that could provide clues, or guideposts as to the direction of my life. I started noticing that if I listened differently, my inner self would hear differently and have a different understanding— a different Knowing of what to do next.

Courage and Surrender

I've been working with a client named Ryan for the last few years. He's in the Software as a Service (SaaS) space. 'Solutions for things in software' is how I describe it.

Chapter 6 – The Shadow

While I have had to analyze what I need to change based on my behaviours for addictions, not all of my clients go through the same things, especially when it comes to business. Some have to look at what they are unwilling to change, and what patterns they've been repeating. The other piece is around comparison and trying to chase the same prize. The tech space and the start-up space are plagued with competitive fear-based chases for money, mentorship, or acquisition. It's a lot of 'lottery thinking,' or conditional thinking. Things like, "If I win then…" or "If this happens, then this can happen…".

It's like surrender, but it's giving up. Not giving in.

It's easy to stay stagnant.

It's easy to just stay in the same lane, making a rut of sorts.

Which is fine, unless people start to complain about it.

Ryan and I met at a conference for transformation. It was ok, but the leader proved to be someone who lied, and lacked integrity, and copied others' content and delivered it as her own. A few of us stayed in touch, and as Ryan built his business, we'd check in with each other. When he was ready, he asked for some insight as to how he could shift his perspective to what was in front of him. He wanted to feel more connected to his business. He was running away on golf trips many times a year to numb out and disconnect from not wanting to face his life here. His social media presented like his life was all fine and good.

The first few retreats I ran were only for women. Ryan always asked why there weren't any men's events for things he wanted to do—self work, nature connection, ties to business, and growth.

I offered Ryan a one-on-one at a private lodge in the Rocky Mountains. We did a 5km hike around the snow-covered trails of Emerald Lake. We'd stop at the benches, making metaphors for the things we see relevant to where we were in our life. Mountain peaks, summits, losing the trail in the snow, creeks and streams coming from the middle of rock-giving life, and things frozen in time until the season is right.

Then he had an ah-ha moment. He stopped on the trail and zoned out. He looked at a mountain and finally, it made sense to him. The answers to his questions came to him. He could see where he was and where he needed to go. He could map out the way there.

He reported to me a 250% increase in the next quarter in his business. He had more confidence. He saw it from another perspective. He knows what his Nest is—the Nest is where he retreats now. This past fall he went on a retreat on his own, for professionals like himself. He travelled to the west coast of Canada and did the next level of work for himself. He came to my office not long ago, talking about new mentors he has, new things he's applying to his business, how he views people and staff, and how he leads.

He's ok not comparing to everyone else.

He's ok not to be in the same chase.

He's found his people.

He's building his life his way, according to his goals and values.

Tina is a Chief Technology Officer whose teenage son decided he wanted to live with his dad and the new girlfriend full-time and go to school away to play academy-level hockey. As he was her only child, Tina was gutted. It's a death—death of the time you thought you would have with someone. Death of a joyous, happy life compared to other families whose kids are living at home.

After Tina's divorce, her faith and trust were shaken.

She was co-parenting with a cold ex and his girlfriend, who lived in a cozy family home where her son spent 50% of his time. As a Type A, high-achieving woman, it's only natural that her son would absorb those traits and apply them to academics and sports. So, at sixteen, he was chosen for academy-level sports, and would move away to board and train. Tina asked to see me one weekend when he asked her not to come visit, because his dad was coming too, and her son wanted to just be with them.

She was devastated.

Chapter 6 – The Shadow

It's at that breaking point that women come to see me, when all the degrees and MBA's and conferences and working your way up feels useless. They come to me when they feel the deepest sense of rejection and grief and loneliness they've ever felt. And even though your child is acting from a place of love, not knowing how deep it cuts, it still does. And, as a professional woman and professional mom, she smiled and acknowledged on the video call that he was allowed to choose that and to have fun, but that it still cut like a knife to the heart. It's the kind of pain that, when the call ends, it makes you keel over into a deep whale cry, and then want to scream and throw something.

This feeling of not liking the way life went, and not liking how it is now, but having to raise children in it, is hard—children who choose pathways we've never heard of, and children who voice the preferences, and choices, and changes they want to make. This feeling of resentment at what is and was, and the anger at what is, and the fear over how it goes from this point forward is out of your control. Then it's a decision put to the group, and the outcome is one to accept and respect.

But that doesn't mean it's easy. It doesn't mean it doesn't hurt.

It doesn't mean that we don't have to check in, and dive deep, and feel into it.

It means we just have to look harder at what it's trying to show us, and get to the Nest to hear the next steps.

A group of women from a mom's group came to one of my retreats. They were members of the group that hosted a wild fun group of women who longed for the hilarity of summer camp to last forever. Their events revolve around badges and booze—and laughing so hard you cry. Often. And you can cry there. You can shed there. You can get really honest about your resentments there.

But they were burnt out. Their lives with their sweet little boys and girls (all high-needs youth) are pendulums that swing to the side of hell on a whim. Their children have intense diagnoses that make them rage from the inside. Sometimes the police are called. Sometimes they're admitted to the psych ward for weeks at a time. Sometimes they hurt family members and siblings. Sometimes it's really bad. These women had each other, but they all came with tired eyes and tired souls. They didn't know how to have a life for themselves. They didn't know how to take time for themselves when they were called to the school, and playdates, and grandparents' houses to pick up their children—constantly.

These women need retreat. These families need retreat. The healthcare system leaves them feeling completely broken, with no support other than signing their guardianship rights away and letting someone else take care of it. None of them wanted this, and none of them knew what to do.

When I was working with them, I was visualizing a healing centre where families can come for respite, have their own space but be on same property, get specific care for their children, get sleep, get counselling, and get retreat.

Each woman left the three days wider-eyed and hopeful. Hopeful that with a shift in their own perspectives of acceptance that what they've been dealt is hard, *very hard*, and a truth that the cages they've been putting themselves in are a bit of a hook to the wrong side of the pendulum. That they are just so tired and fed up that they have said 'fuck-it' to a lot of things. That after having courage and more courage, the scope of a new path to co-create something else feels like there is no energy to get started.

One exercise I suggested to the women at the retreat was a silent walk in nature. If you usually take the path, go off-path. If you usually wander, try a straight line. If you feel like you always walk quickly looking down, try walking slower and look up. If you don't ever walk without earbuds or headphones or a podcast, go in silence. Listen for wind and water and animal chirps.

They did this and one woman reported back that she was so torn about her choices. She usually stays on the path, and this time she went the other way. She usually does what's in flow, and

Chapter 6 – The Shadow

this time she went against the current. She said she didn't like it, and it felt uncomfortable, like she was out of control—and then through tears (breakthrough) she realized that's what she needs to equip her next leg of this journey in motherhood.

Yet, they did see it. And they did believe it. And they did start.

It starts with wanting to start.

And those who come see the others who are plagued in fear, with ego over work, and roles, and titles, fuck-its, comparison, measuring up, fitting into boxes, and the like.

Having the courage to surrender is making a decision to change and identifying the clues and coincidences that will help push us to a new growth place, and a new direction. This is where we feel the spiritual two-hand shove again.

We do this by analyzing our behaviours and thoughts.

Journaling is my way of doing this.

Then I observe what actions came out of my journaling.

Then I can see how I wrote myself to be the hero in the story of life lessons.

How I listened for one-liners to take away, reflect on, and write on, repeated over and
over.

We have to write the things that happen to us, and how we got through them.

We have to document where we were compared to where we are going—data for the
soul.

We have to see if we like that process, or if we would change something.

This is the same thing a business does when it analyzes its activities and profits year over
year.

For some, sadly, it ends there.

The shadow is too hard and dark to get through.

The pain is too much.

There is no more wind in the wings to take flight again.

Sadly, we all know someone who made it here, and we ask, 'Why couldn't they have just have seen another way? Why couldn't they just turn it around?'

I don't know.

But what I do know is that we have to try harder. Have conversations sooner. Go deeper and help each other level up. Analyze the data of our souls without judgment, rather than put people into boxes. We need to listen differently. We need to create more space to let people (especially men) be in this place of having a voice again and saying what they are forcing, and instead peel back some layers and get into feeling. Out of paralyzing ego, into harmonious ego.

Chapter 7 – Logic & Intuition

Hysterectomy
Through reading 32 years of my journals in the first year of the lockdown, a newly single 40-year-old woman who just had a ravenous yet necessary hysterectomy, I felt a physical manifestation of all the pain in my life manifested into my female organs finally go. It was taken from me. I wrote that a "black bowling ball of misery of my past was taken, gone." The scars that manifested into cysts and cells that looked funny. The hysterectomy took away the stored cellular memory and all the pain I felt physically, mentally, sexually, spiritually, and emotionally.

From that void, I grew.

The Knowing it had to go. The logic it had to go. The harmony in the healing.

Suddenly, I was questioning all things about my femininity, my sexuality, myself as a mother, myself as a partner, myself as an entrepreneur who found herself often consulting or teaching or writing by herself.

I made some frightening discoveries about where I learned these patterns and behaviours.

How I repeated them for years.

I was now being given a gift to do some analytical psychology on myself, and in virtual counseling sessions with Artur, I could really dive into the process of how I got myself to where I found myself, and what I was going to do about it.

I was now at a familiar place, questioning religion and organized belief systems, because as the patterns of my past have shown me, when I feel most alone or lonely is when I want to turn back to my false inner self and self-guide and self-direct somewhere dark, or shadowy, or toxic, or unhealthy, or void-like. But I was also at a new place, questioning psychology.

The absolute gift of being able to read my journeying through this pathway set out in my journals showed me what I taught myself, what I had seemingly conformed to, and that I was able to easily choose to move forward differently.

This didn't come without boatloads of tests, lessons, dark places rising up in me, and that void wanting to suck me back in. Temptations and lusty situations, some morally wrong, rose to test my commitment to this journey to not do what I'd done before.

Newly single, I was constantly getting the question, "Have you met anyone?" I hadn't, and wasn't looking. What was around me was more of the same of what I had, and while I didn't want to repeat the journey I already took, I also had no idea what I wanted. I continued to put one foot in front of the other in my Blundstones and lumberjack fleece plaid jacket and let people assume I was gay, as one courageous hockey mom shared with me after hearing the rumours. That's an easier resolve than explaining that I have no idea where I am and what I'm looking for, wandering around again like an odd duck of sorts.

Only, I didn't feel I was an odd duck.

I knew I was flying in a new air stream, reaching new heights in my analysis of myself.

Right before the hysterectomy, I was 'dating' or seeing an old acquaintance—he was older. It felt like a secret relationship, and it was. And it was also an old pattern, and an old behaviour of mine. Being less than. The men who I let harm me, leaving scars on my uterus, were people I let in who weren't safe. This person was the same, as his priority wasn't to make me safe. When I got the surgery, I didn't see him again for over two months. A few weeks before, he gave me a gorgeous birthday dinner, custom cake, sapphire bracelet, and I felt like a queen. And then I felt discarded. I chose someone who love-bombed me, who wasn't rooted in their values as I wasn't rooted in mine.

Chapter 7 – Logic and Intuition

I needed the experience to feel that again, that feeling of going out again and reviving that side of my life. But I also needed to be on a new path with a new flock. Finding that mate for life. That Owl to share a Nest with, moving away from what I didn't want to have.

I didn't want the mask I had been wearing to conform to the story that behind every matching-outfit-family-photo on the front of our annual Christmas cards were truly happy individuals.

That illusion of what happiness is started to crumble, like a castle built on sand.

It's easy to throw in the towel and do what's been done before. It's easy to let our thoughts default on what have become beliefs and make them our new (and old) operating systems that create patterns and pathways and destinations. I know, I've done it over and over and over. This is the 'fuck-its' and it's what kept me stuck in addiction for many years.

Why?

Fear.

Fear tells us that taking the route we've taken before, or one that everyone else is conforming to, is the way. Fear is protecting us from the world around us, telling us to stay quiet and sheltered and look like everyone else. It's what comparison and doubt and jealousy thrive on—feeding from low hanging fruit.

Knowings is knowing we are made up of not just the body, but also the soul. It is something tangible, but also intangible.

What do I mean here? Well, quantum physics shows us some things about energy. Remember that we started this book saying it's about energy. We have to get clear on this point to move through the method, because it's important to see that what we move through is nothing to get something.

Let me explain.

The physical and emotional body is composed of so many seen and unseen things, things that only radio microscopes can measure—cells and DNA and atoms and protons and neutrons and electrons that all have jobs but are difficult to completely understand. Theories that were deemed absolute, like 'DNA can't change,' are being proven wrong by theories that show different outcomes.

That's the world with Knowings in it. It's a little bit different, feels a little different, and allows us to act a little different. We can't help but change because we've been thinking about change.

The physical body, while composed of cells, can be broken down into tiny parts making up a whole. The whole is something seen, our bodies. So, if the body is composed of unseen things now seen, our thoughts can do that too. At that point, we can't put it under a microscope anymore, just like a thought.

But thoughts become things.
Things become beliefs and truths.
Things we can't see influence the physical realm.
This is what I'm talking about.
This is Knowings—where the mind and the spiritual self are seemingly invisible moving forces that impact these cells in the physical body.

Some might say that it just is what it is. It's invisible energy from our mind that shapes our body, our relationships, our connections, our work, and our healing.

How?
Thoughts become things.
Things become beliefs and truths.
Beliefs and truths become our values.
Values become our roots, to ourselves.

Our roots become the new growth for a plan. Our shift in perspective gives us the courage to keep moving towards the plan, through the new plan, not allowing ourselves to get stuck in old blocks and patterns and easy route things.

Radical Honesty
The book *Reveal* changed my life.

"You will have to find the journey, pilgrimage, or spiritual practice that will forge a meeting with the soul-voice inside you. You will have to go through your own discernment process to

Chapter 7 – Logic and Intuition 99

distinguish the voice of fear from the voice of love. The veil that lifts is this: there will never be a voice outside of you that is wiser than your soul-voice or holds more authority over what is best for you. You need guidance and support not to follow someone else's truth but to remain loyal to your own." (Meggan Watterson, *Reveal: A Sacred Manual for Getting Spiritually Naked.*)

I read about a woman with a higher degree from Harvard who is a theologian and writes about everything I've ever felt about the story of the Bible and how so much of it feels wrong. How there is missing information and, historically, things were changed for political benefit or taxation agreements. She was brutally honestly about what she feels, and what signs she notices. She wrote about her pilgrimages to listen inside caves and follow pathways others before us have followed. She's following a remembering.

It gave me permission to feel what I was feeling. To know that what I'm feeling isn't crazy. To know that my deepest desire is to live in love and not be bound by attachments or chains to fear, or control, or resentment, or dependency, or 'doctrines of telling' dogma that make the communities smaller and smaller, not wider and greater. A lot of people come to see me for permission—permission to follow a thought or a hunch or a sign and explore what else there is. They know that a world of doing what we've always done is not all there is.

Danielle LaPorte wrote *The Desire Map* years ago about tuning into how you want to feel over what you need to do. It came into my life at a time when I was desperate to be seen and relevant in the work world, and I was in a women's group processing all of these 'who am I' questions rising up. I was with other women who were being brutally honest about the markers ten years down the road from where I was if I stayed on that path and didn't tune into what I was feeling. These women walked with me through the finding myself and losing myself and finding myself again, the journey we were all on. It meant going against the grain of the world a little bit, and letting life happen at the same time. Babies, teenagers, stay-at-home mom work, single woman in her 40s with no kids life, divorce, job changes, societal patterns of hierarchy and patriarchy, and how they just feel wrong.

Being able to be radically honest is being able to hear yourself, first.

When you're guided by a new light, a new source, you're guided with love.

When you're radically honest with yourself, things coming to your mind or to your lips and off your tongue will surprise you. Not so much 'Did I just say that out loud?' as 'Oh shit, now I have to actually do it.'

Radically honesty is about the fact that you'll have to change.

You'll have to choose to change.

Choose to make a decision to identify the fear, push through your ego, have the courage to take a leap of faith on a new pathway that you feel is right, and tune into your Knowing that it aligns with your values, and you trust it. Then you choose to be on the pathway to change.

The choice to change will come with all kinds of temptations that you will face.

Thoughts that go against what is on your path.

People coming and offering other things.

Job offers or raises in salaries to stay in a role you know you can do, but isn't for you.

Staying in a relationship where you have one foot out and are unwilling to put two feet in.

Nudges to change your university program—moving out of what others expect of you, and moving into what you know you're called to do.

Saying no to that arranged marriage or career to appease others as you know it will set you up for a life of living hell.

Picking your poison is something you'll do for the rest of your life.

You'll be faced with things that tempt the path you tell yourself you're on.

Chapter 7 – Logic and Intuition

What's you're poison? Whatever you give power to, or make an idol, or feel dependency to.

- You'll try to eat healthy, and you'll be temped with travel and food and things to take you off-track.
- You'll want to leave your work and make a story that you can't because of a money dependency.
- You'll want to have hard conversations in your relationships and always hold back your truth to keep their peace, only giving you an inner hell feeling.
- You'll want to book a trip away to explore a part of yourself, and your values—adventure, connection to ocean, hiking a wonder of the world, conquering a challenge of landing on each continent, etc. But meanwhile, you put all the blame on other people and things in your life as the reason you can't go.
- You'll feel a big shift in your connection to spirit and feel too much shame to tell people you're exploring it and trying new practices.
- You'll want to speak your truth, but instead you live a lie for years, if not decades.

When you say 'no' to others, you say 'yes' to yourself.

Being able to hear yourself is about a new level of self-care and self-protection. Safety is key in all of this work. Many dive in and go fast—too fast. They want all the feelings and shifts and miracles to happen all at once. Instead, they get a spiritual hangover of sorts and are more lost and more confused, while sometimes what the body needs is periods of deep rest. I see many chase teachers and destinations, thinking they'll find their fix there, only to find that everywhere they go, they still feel that sense of uncertainty and loss and loneliness—just somewhere else.

Yoga in the west is a chase for the best body and longest handstand, whereas eastern practices are about tuning in differently. When I was in India for the first time at age eighteen, a woman wanted to practice yoga with me and insisted I be at her house before sunrise, at 4 a.m. I was to bike in the dark on dirt roads with no streetlights in Ghandinagar in Gujurat so I could practice yoga. I was still in a mindset that yoga was for the body and a physical change would ensue, not realizing the work was in the practice of getting there before sunrise and staying committed to that practice, and growing from there. Young minds want fast rewards. I didn't have the courage to see it differently then. I was only listening to the ego of my desire, not the real pathway to transformation and change.

Signs

Once, in my first year of university, I was in a meeting for a volunteer group when a woman took a call on a flip cell phone. It was her daughter who nannied in France the year before, and was asking if the mom knew anyone who could go this year. The mom put her hand over the mouthpiece and asked our small group. On a hunch I said that I would, and I signed up right there. I got the family's number and within a few weeks, it was organized. My dad was a pilot, so getting flights was as easy as signing up for a pass.

On my way there I stopped in Montreal and, walking past a collection of payphones, a man called to me to ask if I knew how to use them. His French accent was thick, obviously not French Canadian. He told me he was headed to Calgary (my city) for university, and I told him that after a summer in France, I would be back. I taught him how to put a quarter into the phone and we went on our way. When we met again, we became fast friends. He was much younger, but fun. He came to my family's house for dinner and we would laugh about the Canadian ways.

The next summer, I wanted to head back to France and he called his parents and arranged that I could stay at their house in Paris, and come and go as I please. It was wonderful. I was young and curious, and people wanted to show me around and take me out. I had morning café au lait in a sunroom kitchen in a home

Chapter 7 – Logic and Intuition

hundreds of years old full of souvenirs and worldly things. It was colourful and chic, historical and new to me. Following the sign of his call led to a years-long connection, and we still chat today about his record label, EnSoul, and all the things he's up to now.

If I didn't follow the sign or clue of the woman who asked if anyone was interested in going, I wouldn't have led myself to that amazing journey of a few years living and working back and forth from Europe.

Ms. Baxter told me to order a book called *Messengers of Light*. In the pages of that book I learned that you could write to spirits, or people on the other side. On the other side were people who died, or crossed over. In that book, you can write letters to people and communicate in that way. You can ask for things, or ask for signs.

Another psychic taught me to ask for things—like a sign of a yellow duck if my plans and my pathway are aligned for what I desire, and to understand that it might come as a toy, or a picture, or a picture in a kid's book, or a text that mentions 'yellow duck.' This isn't testing God or challenging in a 'show me or I won't believe' kind of way. No, that's forcing and controlling the outcome. This is about surrendering that you don't know it all, and don't know the way, and need to look for clues.

People are scared of death. They are scared of the unseen and unknown. It's easier to believe in a place that sounds nice than an 'I don't know' place. It's easier not to think about it. But not thinking about it makes people sick. It makes people unable to zoom out and see a bigger picture and a new perspective on death, loss, and grief. People who come to see me around death stuff carry so much fear and shame about what they did, or what they said, and letting that go is very hard.

I had a woman approach me at a retreat when she was finally ready to talk. She had lost her mom and her dad in the past year, and the last time she saw her mom, she hadn't said goodbye as she thought she should. She hadn't said goodbye as though it were the last goodbye. She was carrying that guilt for a whole year about what she couldn't change and couldn't fix, until she shifted her perspective and saw it differently. She could fix it, because she could fix herself. She could fix it, because she could write a better ending than that one.

Often, we tell ourselves something is the way it has to be, when that's a lie. We can tell a better story. We can tell a better ending. We can tell a story more on legacy and remembering than on the one thing that didn't happen. She needed a sign to know that's what it was. She heard me talk about death and life and grief, and how acknowledging grief is a monster we need to tame, and when we do, it's mean monster things, it's unpredictable, and it follows no logical process. It's feeling down, feeling sad, feeling longing, crying randomly, conversations in our head we didn't have, and thoughts that can send us on spin cycles to keep us stuck in what isn't' true. The truth is that we can grow in it. The truth is that we can grow from it.

Knowings is essentially about feelings, seeing, hearing, and knowing the signs. Signs come to us in all different ways. In the metaphysical world there are different levels of what the French call *'clair'* or *clairaudience* for clearly hearing, or *clairvoyant* for clearly seeing, or *clairsentience* for feeling, or *claircognizance* for knowing.

At times, people see signs through animals or other things in nature which are able to connect us back to a remembering of things from our consciousness. We can find meanings from these intimate connections between ourselves and the patterns of nature, and the animal kingdom and how they grow, and survive, and struggle, and adapt, and go through all the same things that we going through in the human experience.

We also sometimes see in the patterns of nature what it looks like to be wild versus what it looks like to be domesticated. We have animals that we've chosen to domesticate, or wild animals that we get very close to and earn their trust. At the same time, this is where the pieces of what true nature is shows us what can come out in a wild animal that's been domesticated.

Here is an example of the seven stages of the Knowings method showing up when my son Cooper was attacked by a dog.

It was a lot of fear around feeling the pain of seeing the

Chapter 7 – Logic and Intuition

physical pain of my child and then having to put our egos aside between dog owner (my brother and Cooper's uncle) and myself as a mother and caregiver and the person communicating and surrendering to the outcome with the authorities when bylaw and social services and Calgary Police got involved.

There was that intuitive Knowing that I needed to stand up for my child and protect other children because of the unknown nature of the wildness that was this dog. This didn't come without going to consult with other people who had familiarity with dog behaviour. I got my advice, and at the same time, I slipped back into pride and ego.

My brother got his own advice. We then had a difficult conversation when it came down to the animal rescue agency wanting to take the dog back and go through its own pride and ego process of saving a dog's life and rehabilitating it, even when I had an intuitive Knowing that this was something beyond being domesticated and trained. This was something that had to go back to its wild nature.

This was such a hard process of forgiveness, grace, and love of being in a family and understanding that my brother's family had lost its family pet—the most devastating feeling that something's been taken away—this object and symbol of love. It's also the hardest to understand and get to the place of feeling how my brother's family must have felt going through all the motions of the kids losing a pet, not understanding, and not being able to reveal all the details.

When Cooper was healing, he wanted to see the dog again because he couldn't imagine that the attack would happen again. In his little innocent eyes and innocent world, dogs wouldn't do that.

We all must understanding that sometimes things flip; sometimes things challenge us; sometimes things are very hard to come to middle ground or find a dialogue between two pieces. But we are never without going through this cycle of fear, to pride, to courage, to Knowings, to forgiveness, to grace, to love. We then come back to the Nest every single time, at the heart of the Knowing, and either accept and forgive ourselves for the decisions we've made, or accept and stand in the decisions that we've made. Either way, we have to push forward knowing that taking this as a life experience and having that intuitive journey will move us and others forward.

Sometimes people believe that animals come as a spirit guide, or something sent from the other side to teach us things. I am on the fence with this belief system. I believe we can get information about ourselves from observing patterns of nature, but I don't know for sure if there's a deeper connection. It's not something I was raised around nor does my body naturally root or anchor into this idea—spirit guide or spirit animal. But just because it's not for me doesn't make it untrue. I'm just not the teacher for it. I am more the student of animal behaviour and the mysteries around how they are and what they know.

I have been shown the power of the animal spirit. Do they have souls? I'm not sure. Do they have spirit? Absolutely. Do they have a wild animal nature as well? Absolutely.

Susan's dog, Abby, communicated with me and this brought me to love animals, and feel for the pain of animals in a way I was never taught to do as someone who was never raised with a dog. I never knew that connection, that loyalty, that bond, that "man's best friend" so to speak. I knew people had it. I knew people considered their animals like pets. I knew they considered them very close relationships, but I never knew there was a connection as deep as what I was shown through my experience with Abby.

My friend Susan is a horse jumper, and she was away in California on a competition for six weeks. She had someone taking care of the barn and her animals, and while she was gone, I didn't plan on visiting. The farm is a couple kilometres outside of town and I was driving somewhere, and I had to pass the road that turns off toward her farm. As I was going by, I kept hearing an intuitive Knowing, or calling. There were messages coming to me from somewhere else saying, "Turn on the road, go to the farm, turn on the road, go to the farm, turn on the road, go to

Chapter 7 – Logic and Intuition

the farm…" When I hear things three times, or when the repetition comes in groups of three, I know it's serious and I pay attention.

It's also how I can discern within myself what's coming from my logical mind and what's coming from my intuitive self. A huge practice is learning to know the difference and come into a place of being able to discern and differentiate where the messages are coming in, and through us. Are they coming from our connection to our spiritual self, to our spiritual guides, and to that source messaging, or is it coming from our logical mind made up under that veil of concentrated thoughts, spinning here in the world? I knew that this message was coming from my intuitive self because I knew that physically, I had to take action, like something in my body was turning the wheel to go down that road.

When I arrived at the farm, there were open barn doors, and it felt desolate and eerie. Besides the horses in their paddocks outside, no one else was around. Usually when I drive up, the dogs run out the lane and there's some kind of activity from the barn. Not that day.

I walked around, and it almost felt like no one had been there for a while and I noticed some of the behaviours of the horses were not calm, not natural. They were not just grazing in the paddock. One of them was going back and forth, back and forth, almost gnawing at the railing, exhibiting some signs of deep stress and discontent.

When I went over to the horses, one tried to nip at me, and my first intuitive thought was that it must be hungry. I continued to wander around and I really couldn't shake the feeling. I didn't know where the dogs were, and I started calling out more and more.

I made my way into the garage where the dog beds and food were. I didn't see any remnants of water or food either, and I knew something was seriously wrong. I was trying to contact my friend but she was in competition so there was a gap between us being able to communicate. I heard a whimpering at the bottom of the stairs from the four-car garage that has a cold, concrete floor with one door leading into the house and one leading into the basement, almost like access to a separate suite. At the bottom of about fifteen concrete steps that go down to the basement entrance was the dog Abby, and she was laying on the concrete floor shaking; she looked very weak, and very frail.

But there was something in the connection of her eyes looking up at me that communicated with me, "Oh, I called you here." That was the first time in my life that I experienced feeling the sign from an animal, and hearing the call, and being able to come across kilometres of fields and roadways to get to what the animal needed.

Abby ended up going to the clinic where she was put on various steroids, and it was brought to our attention that she had an autoimmune disease, and something that now required steroids and medication for her day-to-day. In that, there are miracles in more than one way of finding life. Discovering something that keeps you alive is also a miracle, not just a miraculous cure.

Abby communicating with me on the highway was a miracle.

I have had a connection with Abby since that day that has transcended through love. This dog can communicate with me, and she took away my fear of dogs after the attack with Cooper. She took away my pride and ego of thinking that I know that there's one way to communicate with animals. It gave me the courage to step into understanding and reading some stories that other people have had about their intuitive connections with animals, and believing in that side that some people can communicate with them. I also know there's an innate, wild nature to animals and we have to love them, but with boundaries all the same.

I've had to go through a journey of self-forgiveness and having the grace to dive in and unlearn and change my thoughts of what I thought I knew about animals, and how they can't communicate, and how we have this kind of authority over them.

Chapter 7 — Logic and Intuition

Yes, we do have to have an authority over them when it comes to proper training. It's the same with ourselves and relationships—we have to have boundaries. But we also can connect differently, and this is something that when we are open to learning a new way, the signs, the symbols, and the things that are here to show us another message will start to appear more frequently.

Many people believe that synchronicities are something we need to pay attention to, and I agree. Others use terms such as coincidence, fate, destiny, divine timing, answered prayers, miracles, and messages sent from (fill in the blank). We get the opportunity to call it what we want. So, whether the signs come to us through symbols, objects, feelings, visions, or auditory messages, it doesn't matter. But what we need to do is be aware of all the different ways that the signs come in, and then open ourselves to pay attention to them.

Chapter 8 – It's In You

The Intuition Perspective
As a kid who grew up reciting the Lord's Prayer before school, standing at my desk as the loudspeaker squawked into each classroom, usually with some blip from the secretary at the start, I would say it, day after day, and feel nothing. Memorized religion has no spirit. It wasn't until years later that I broke down what the prayer was, when it was written, and for whom, and how it became some kind of spiritual war declaration we arm our children with before their prescribed learning in a school system that has boxes in boxes in boxes of bureaucracy attached to it.

Two phrases hit me in my late 30s as phrases I've heard 1000 times, yet that time I heard it differently.

"Love thy neighbor as thyself."

and

"Forgive others and their trespasses as we forgive those who trespass against us."

Huh.

Full stop.

If I break these two down, turns out it's a me thing—'...as thyself' and '...as we forgive.'

Both of those imply that I do it first. I do *me* first.

For two decades I'd been seeking in a logical way how the outer world could show me how to do it first. I'd been wearing masks and trying to fit into boxes of how others did it. I was listening to them. I wasn't listening from the Nest.

Now that I knew how to listen differently, the things I was instructed to do were harder, and harder to lean into. Read those old journals, write that book, say that declaration of love, let go of what's not holding onto you, have confidence you can do this on your own. Things like that. And the more I did, the greater the reward within me felt, and the 'as thyself' was manifesting into something great—something I was living and exploring and writing about at the same time. Like being my own test subject. That's analytical journaling and reflection.

The 'as thyself' meant no more stories keeping me cages.

It meant no more fear-based thinking, fear-based things around me (yes, some friendships have to go), realizing where I'm giving more than receiving in relationships, and reflecting on whether I'm not expressing my truth and being honest.

It meant reflecting on where my ego was ruffling my feathers and others, or was life-giving and a lesson learned to grow from. When my feathers are up, so is my tone. I come across as more aggressive and harsh, not assertive and helpful. I reflected on speaking from a scared place and trying to defend myself, rather than expressing that I was weary about co-creating.

It meant writing out plans one, two, and three, and having the courage to look at and feel through all the scenarios. Maybe the best one for me wasn't the one I thought it was, and maybe an outcome can surprise me. This exit from the cage meant that I had to look at where I was comfortable feeding my unhelpful ego before, and just setting the stage to stay status quo. Playing house. Playing a role in a marriage and a home.

It meant turning to that inner voice for guidance, not whatever informed my mindless scrolling.

It meant surrendering that I actually don't know the way forward, and that's ok, as feeling lost is better than feeling caged.

It meant believing that a feeling of transforming from what didn't work to what will is something I have to keep my eye and attention focused on. I have to show up halfway. It meant that the work on creating the vision, and flying over it, and checking in on it was something I had to do over and over. I had to show up and stand in the possibility of the vision and writings I had and shift my thoughts and believe I could glow differently, just like that golden tree. Just like I imagined I could.

Chapter 8 – It's In You

I had to use my old tools (writing) and do some work (prompting and guiding) and that's what's created the last section of this book. You'll write your way to your heaven and your hell; you'll write your values and life and career plans. You'll write your next steps, aligned with a vision, aligned with a plan, aligned with a new light within you illuminating the way.

The point of learning the Knowings program and understanding the flow of the method is that we can take our healing into our own hands and create a sacred space for it; a safe space for it. We come to understand that the three highest principles of forgiveness, grace, and love are co-created with a power greater than us; a source we identify when we retreat to the Nest. For some, this source can be the spirituality that remains from a religion they walked away from, and for others this source can be a spark in their religion, or belief system, that is identified in doctrines and representative archetypes, and it's what they as an organized group or community believe and follow. These groups are comfortable connecting and following the same doctrine that may or may not have been passed down and transcribed and translated many different times since its conception.

There's great comfort and safety in organized groups and communities that believe in the Knowings principles, which appear in many faiths and traditions and belief systems. Stories and myths and oral traditions and references in the Bible, and the Koran, and the Hindi texts, all referenced the theme of fear, and pride, and courage. And the characters exercise acts of forgiveness, and grace, and love in their own ways.

There's more that unites us than divides us.

And the Knowings Method extracts these core principles and cross-checks them with different faiths, and traditions, and belief systems, and extracts what's good. Extracting what's good is important in shaping our language in an affirming way, and equally important is having a practice of healthy self-talk that encourages and empowers our self-confidence, and our self-image, and our self-assessment that we do each day.

Intuition – I intuit

Intuition is feelings over facts. We listen for that inner guidance, that inner compass, that inner Knowing to show us the signs that we trust so we can move in a direction that's aligned with our values. We accept that we've done the work, evolving ourselves and co-creating with that power that recharges us in the Nest. A big piece of pushing through the Knowings Method and getting to a place of being, and feeling, and knowing, and doing differently is changing the way we speak, and changing the environment around us, and changing what we listen to, and changing what we said before. Co-creating a new path forward for ourselves and shifting the direction that we thought we were going to go can be scary.

Learning how to use the map of Knowing with the OwlSeek Method is simple. By using the downloadable visual tool, you can see a way to connect your thoughts and experiences with where you're at now, and design the place you ultimately want to be, using the goals that you have, the actions you want to put in place, and the things you're moving towards right now. You'll aim to get to a place of growth that attracts a higher perspective in yourself, connecting you to new environments, new literature, new mentors, new teachers in new classes, new thought theories on whatever you're looking into, being able to discern within your body what direction you need to take. The most stagnant thing and the most stagnant place for ourselves is to be stuck as a state of mind first, and then a physical walk in our body and a physical block from our intuitive connected self. The whole point of Knowings and turning it into a verb, 'I Intuit,' is connecting to that intuitive, living verb part of yourself where you can take action.

How do you Intuit? You go to the Nest—that metaphorical place that you can go when you close your eyes and take three deep breaths, and you listen to your body differently before you listen to your head. Then you connect the dots. But it's being able to get to a place where you feel those two things are connected again, through three deep breaths.

Chapter 8 – It's In You

With those three deep breaths, when you open your eyes, you need to set your eyes on a new intention, or a new motivation, or new goal. By doing that, connect to the higher perspective words and you are able to create new thoughts that become your beliefs, that become new things that move you forward, that become new goals you start, that become the actions you take, that become new experiences and things you can tangibly hold.

Forgiveness
Forgiveness is co-creation, that combination of two things, the surrendering and the letting go; it's two parts. Forgiveness is us knowing what forgiveness is, and feeling what forgiveness is. To say, "I forgive, but I don't forget," is to say that you logically understand forgiveness, but you don't feel it. That's not true forgiveness, and that doesn't create that heart centred place. That peace of feeling forgiveness takes us to a place that's more harmonious with our mind and our self—that is, our mind and our soul self. We feel more inspired and inspiring when those two pieces come together.

Self-forgiveness is one of the hardest lessons to learn. It's one of the hardest things to come around to after cheating or staying too long, and after lying or not being authentic.

Grace
Grace is one of the hardest levels to understand because it involves feeling differently and trusting that feeling differently is from Knowing that surrendering at the level of forgiveness is what we have to logically do to have our body feel differently. Being in a state of grace is a transformational place where we become peacefully aware that things just are, and it's not all about us, and we absolutely are not the ones in control, and it feels inspiring. We start to act with more intentionality because life has meaning and purpose. Things that we've put in place to help

move us forward and rebuild (like boundaries) start to feel good.

Grace is a state of feeling—it's just feeling differently. We are grateful. We feel differently. We accept that it comes from a different place. We have this body sensation, that kind of shiver that is a little bit intense, but also comforting. We just start to see things differently, and act from a place of being more serene, and having more bliss in our life, and more quietude, and not needing to cast our opinion or judgment or prejudice on anything.

Love

And then we start to feel the tiny miracles happen. Every day, there's some time during the day where we just know that we're in flow. And whatever we surround ourselves with in our environment starts to feel different. We know it's working. We put the right people in place to help us through this, and we start to ask ourselves how we didn't see it before.

When we're living from a place that's more love-centred, we can't help but be more compassionate and understand that life is about giving and receiving.

From here, we can easily identify the difference between a caged leader through force and fear, versus someone who shares the power of the brilliant leadership by illuminating and helping others shine.

Credo/Values

Knowings is where we create a credo for how we co-create and how we know we're aligning with some certainty in our decisions and desires, and moving towards our goals and dreams with actions and plans.

The credo is a roadmap and guiding light—the guiding principles, so to speak—for each individual.

A credo is the statement of your personal belief, aligning your values that guide you when you're making decisions to remind yourself of the place you want to act from. It can also

Chapter 8 – It's In You

help you be more disciplined, or structured, or organized in how you want to move forward with your own actions, decisions, and behaviours. This can help us move in the direction we want to go for our personal adventures, as well as our professional endeavours.

Putting time and intentionality and focus into this can help create a sense of purpose and meaning in aligning what we do with who we are. The credo is checking in with who we are with the prompts that have been created by the Knowings Method and the OwlSeek Method.

The beauty in these prompts and answers is that they're very personal, and will vary from person to person. Choosing to make meaningful and purposeful decisions and actions in our life takes some guidance, and we need to reflect on our values and beliefs, and check in and see if these are aligned with how we want them to be, or if we need to add a few more.

The origin of the word *credo* is Latin and it comes from the verb *credere*, which means to believe or to trust. This is about us trusting our word with ourselves. The greatest outcome of getting through the method is that we do what we said we're going to do, and we align and do it.

Christian groups have organized themselves and created creeds to put statement to their belief systems. In more organized structures, credos become doctrine, and this is the accepted set of beliefs or principles that this group or organization believes is true. We often find these in religious and philosophical writing as tenants or sets of beliefs that form the basis of a particular ideology, or system, or process. Principles are things we can set forth for ourselves as fundamental truths or beliefs, and they're kind of like a foundation that we build on. And philosophy becomes a way of thinking or a worldview. These are five different ways that credos have shown up over time: creed, doctrine, tenants, principles, and philosophy.

A credo is deciding your middle on the pendulum.
Start your "what's next" with this:
- Identify each side as your heaven or hell

- Identify your ideal vs. your spin cycle
- Know your Nest and your cage
- Have a willingness to take a higher perspective

The deliverable is **your** credo—your Knowing about your life, wellness, health, work, calling, relationships, and more.

The deliverable is to make plans to seek more support on your journey from others who specialize in what you identify as an area to focus on.

The ask is to make your own symbolism for your Nest, and what you call on there: what you need to heal, how you want to feel, what you want to think, how you'll get there, what you want to change, what you're choosing, what spin cycle you can identify, and what you're willing to shift your perspective on.

Your 'I know' statements are your intuition principles cross-checked so you trust yourself and your challenges ahead. For example, depression, anxiety, stagnancy, settling for less, or acting out in ego are all opportunities to breathe into what's next. Use your logic and your intuition, and ask "What is this?" and then you get your answer.

It's never just one thing that needs to change. You are never done this process. It will be about the "both and" of data and soul, spirituality and logic models of faith, fear, and love, your heaven on earth and hell on earth from the mindsets we create, your cage and your higher perspective on life. It's all in you.

Three Deep Breaths

If you made it this far, thank you! I'm proud of you. It means you read this and reflected on your own life, your own journey, your own pain and suffering, and what you want to do with it. The questions are like to ask those who work with me are;

So What?
Now What?
For What?

Chapter 8 – It's In You

As you go forward, I suggest you reflect on these, too. For everything that's ever happened to you and you feel like you can't let go, I ask you to ask yourself these three questions.

So What?
What happened? What's the problem? Why are you spinning on this?

Now What?
What do you want to happen? What do you want to come from this? Where do you ideally want to be? Why would this be happening, what is needing to shift? How are you taking action moving closer to an ideal life?

For What?
What is the lesson from this? What pattern have you been repeating? What have you been holding onto that needs to just go (story, illusion, people, places, things). How are you going to show up differently, closer to your ideal life and ideal self?

Once you're able to ask yourself these three things everything about the method that is book, The OwlSeek Method, you'll be well on your way to soaring to new heights, or quietly watching the world go by, full of wisdom and knowledge, and not needing to invite the squabble and chaos what was from a time not so long ago.

My hope for you is you've heard something there. My hope for you is you've felt something here. My hope for you is you have healed something here, and remember that nature is free and we all have access around the world to watch, reflect, and see things differently.

I see you. I see you seeing things differently, and I'm so proud of you.

Love Jill

Taking it Forward – Finding Your Knowings

You can download the worksheets at www.owlseek.ca and get started with your own transformation today. Or you can grab your own journal and find a cozy place to make yourself a little Nest and answer each question thoughtfully.

The path forward only requires one thing from you—a choice.

You choose a new way.
You choose to listen differently.
You choose to see life in a new perspective.

Fear/Force – The Cage

1. In my life I am stuck on…
2. In my mind I find myself spinning on…
3. I contribute to my spin cycle by…
4. I keep dark patterns, habits, and/or behaviours alive by…
5. My cage is…
6. My fears are…
7. Things I'm trying to force and control are…
8. Something preventing me from moving forward on my goals is…
9. Words that I use that keep me stuck, stagnant, or spinning are…
10. A nature metaphor for what I feel like my cage or hell on earth would be…

Ego/Pride – The Mask
1. I describe my ego as…
2. To me, pride is…
3. A mask I wear and hide behind is…
4. My feathers are ruffled when…
5. A logical thought that keeps me in my rut and in a spin cycle is…
6. Actions I take that go against how I truly want to feel are…
7. In my life, I am inauthentic with…
8. Things I do to appease others that feel inauthentic to me are…
9. Words that keep me stuck in pride, wearing a mask, and feeling inauthentic are…
10. A nature metaphor that keeps me stuck in righteousness and pride is…

Courage / Surrender – The Shift
1. Beliefs that keep me stuck are…
2. Beliefs of mine that came from other people (parents, grandparents, culture, religion) are…
3. I want the courage to do, feel, and say…
4. The one thing I know I need to push through is…
5. Things in my life (people, places, things, ideas) that need to go are…
6. If I don't let these things go then the impact will be…
7. Things that I want to let into my life (people, places, things, ideas) are…
8. If I don't let these things into my life, the impact will be…
9. Words that help me feel courageous and hopeful are…
10. A nature metaphor that gives me the courage to see another perspective is…

Chapter 8 – It's In You

Knowings – I know I Intuit from my heart
1. Intuition to me is…
2. The Source of wisdom that comes to me is called…
3. The Nest I go to can be described as…
4. My core values are…
5. The activities/people closest to my core values are…
6. My work/management values are…
7. It's important to separate my core values and work values because…
8. I wish I was doing more (of)…
9. Words that describe how I feel when I'm intuitive and in the Nest are…
10. A nature metaphor for where you feel you are right now, in the Nest, would be…

Forgiveness / Surrender – Let Go
1. Forgiveness is…
2. To surrender is to…
3. Co-creation, two things coming together, are me and…
4. Letting go is something I do often by…
5. Thoughts or things I know I need to surrender/let go of are…
6. Calming my central nervous system is done by three deep breaths, and…
7. The seats on the board of directors of my life are named (legal, financial, relationship, career, spiritual, physical health, mental health, etc)…
8. Words that describe the feeling of forgiveness, letting go, and surrender are…
9. A nature metaphor for forgiveness and surrender would be…
10. For me, feeling brilliance in co-creating feels like…

Grace / Transformation – Feel different
1. Grace is…
2. Transformation can be described as…
3. Being in a state of allowing feels like…
4. The main difference of a life led with grace over a life led with ego is…
5. I invite more grace into my life with the practice of…
6. I want grace to be extended to others by (prayers, thoughts, actions)…
7. I need to show more grace towards myself for…
8. I am willing to do more… to receive more…
9. Words that describe grace and transformation are…
10. A nature metaphor for transformation and change would be…

Love / Illumination – Lead from inner brilliance and power
1. Love is…
2. To be illuminated from within feels like…
3. The Source of the illumination comes from…
4. Leading from an inner illuminated place would feel like…
5. Things I want to learn from love are…
6. A higher perspective in love means that…
7. I want more … from love.
8. Self-love means that…
9. Words that describe love to me are…
10. A nature metaphor to describe love and how it feels would be…

Appendix

When my friend died in my arms, the next step was arranging his funeral, something I've never done. I compiled this story with only his stories, my recordings, and some friend testimonies. My hope is it reaches someone in his family, I saved some of his things to share with his roots in Eastern Canada when the day comes. I miss you my friend.

Chuck's Eulogy 2015
I am Jill Drader and I'm a friend of Chuck's. Nine years ago, I moved back to Calgary from South Korea where I went to teach English following university. I taught in Seoul and Busan. After a couple of years away and finding recovery rooms on my journey, my first meeting back in Calgary was Knox Nooner and Chuck was chairing. We connected over Korea and Busan – a port where I stood and learned of Korean War History, and a port he arrived at from Japan when he exited the boat as a night fighter and soldier in 1950. We stood in the same place only fifty-five years apart.

In the last five years, I have helped Chuck with various medical issues. I drove and accompanied him to appointments and specialists. Five years ago, I agreed to be his 'next of kin' when the hospital asked him who his emergency contact would be and he said he had no one, and then turned to me and said, "Could it be you, kid?" I agreed since I knew we will intuitively know how to handle situations which used to baffle us.

For the last seven years, Chuck has called me every day, sometimes up to three times a day, to check in, see how I am, and connect. We would talk of the day, the weather, spirits, Jesus, Sylvia Browne, psychics, prayer, stew recipes, my children and my work, past lives, and the Holy Spirit. He told me, "I'm psychic and so are you, that's why we are friends" – and I believe this to be true. We would drive around Calgary to neighbourhoods he couldn't bike to anymore to talk about memories he had. We went to Banff, a place he hadn't seen. We took my boys to the zoo and parks, and he would be deeply concerned about their rambunctious nature!

He was an intelligent man who did his learning through books. He used to tell the doctors at the hospital, "My life experience is like my vocabulary – limited." This limited vocabulary led to some tough conversations when his diagnosis left him asking me what the words 'cancer, chemotherapy, lymphoma, palliative and hospice' meant. I found immense strength from those in this room today who helped with these tough talks.

Six months ago, I noticed Chuck was changing. His stature, his colour, and his drive. He talked of more pain in his stomach. He was a proud man of his fierce independence having lived alone in an apartment at 8th and 8th for twenty-three years and assured me he was seeing a chiropractor who was helping him through. Little did we know this was when B-cell lymphoma was entering his body and would be what took his last breath. On July 3rd it had been days since I heard from him. I intuitively knew something was wrong. I called for a police check on him and they found him curled up in bed in acute pain. The police called me to come take him to the ER immediately.

We will suddenly realize God is doing for us what we could not do for ourselves. Chuck and the doctors said he would have died in that bed had I not called on him. He thanked me every day for being able to keep him alive a little longer. He had a strong willingness to progress – one like no other I've seen.

Before we got to the RGH ER on July 3rd, Chuck told me he had a dream. A team came and said, "You're wanted in heaven." There was a woman, who looked like me, who took him to the hospital and he never got out. And there was a hospital in a picture, a bright light. It was in the blue and white clouds. That's exactly what happened.

Chuck had unwavering faith that we were connected by a

Appendix

power greater than ourselves. We went from Rocky View to Tom Baker to Carewest Fanning rehab for mobility issues, to Peter Lougheed for respiratory issues, to the Sarcee Hospice to his final resting place here. Before we left for the hospice, he told a couple of guys who came to visit him, "This is where I will go to die." And that he did, less than two hours after arriving. He was unconscious when he arrived at the hospice except for two times he woke up. Once he asked me to change the dim lamp to the bright pot light. It seemed odd. Then he asked me to turn him towards the light. With the help of two nurses, we did. And with that, he was gone again, he went towards the light.

Over the years I have felt an immense presence of his late mother, Alice, around me – in only a way the magic and mystery of the presence of the Holy Spirit can explain. Alice passed away six months after Chuck was born from complications from childbirth. I felt her come to me and say, "Bring my baby home." I took that calling with great honour and today, I lay to rest your baby Alice. Thank you for guiding me here.

We are here today because we know Chuck. My story is not special about my connection with him – rather all ours connected and collaborated are. You know Chuck. You know he biked all year round, swam every morning in the apartment building pool, attended Daily Reflection at 9:30 a.m., had coffee somewhere and lunch at home, went to Knox for noon, biked and jogged near the river before he started making dinner at 4:30 p.m. He stayed in most evenings, lifting weights and listening to CBC talk radio as he had no TV after the bunny ears to hijack cable went out of style. He was usually in bed around 8 p.m.

In July, he took his thirty-three years in the hospital with flowers and cards from the Daily and Knox groups and a cake I brought to share with the nurses and doctors. They came in to congratulate him and talk to him about his experience. Because his experience could benefit the medical team and the patients they treat – and I'm confident that at some point in their careers, they will share the story of a strong-willed man they met battling a mysterious disease and held a strong mind until the end.

When Trina, Todd and I cleaned out his apartment while he was in the hospital, he only asked to hold onto a few sweaters, his radios and alarm clocks with red lights. A simple man. We found his quirky collections, pens from any location where they were given away, books and books and books, and more than 100 pairs of shoelaces stashed around the place and repurposed for hanging and tying things together. And when we didn't know what we were going to do with all his stuff, two new Canadians appeared in front of us and told us they would help others in their community with it.

Chuck likely referred to you with a nickname. I've heard "Mazda for Magda", "Irish" or "French" depending on where you're from, "The Woodsman", "The Lawyer", "The Hot Dog Guy", "The out-of-town oil guy", "The Pilot", "The football players wife", and kiddo, for any woman younger than him.

You may have wrapped gifts with him for Christmas parties or shared a coffee with him at the Sunday morning Ramada meeting. He always had time for a chat, in fact, he valued that time immensely. If you were hurting, he likely told you to focus on the Step 3, 7 or 11, prayers, or he recited a quote or words of encouragement.

He did have a warm soul, he was kind, he cared, he thought about you when you weren't around, and he wondered if those who were hurting were going to be ok. He loved coffee and servers in restaurants along 8th Avenue, where he lived, would respect that he just wanted to sit in their establishments for a warm cup and somehow understood he didn't understand 'tipping'. That being said, he did try to make sure he had something for the 7th tradition either from his own wallet or that of someone else's!

The five lessons I will take away from my friendship with Chuck are:

1. Wool sweaters are the best
2. Pray
3. Speak simply and bold
4. Stay active

Appendix 129

    5. Read recovery literature and attend meetings regularly.

Five years ago, I asked Chuck to tell me his story of his early years. I recorded and transcribed it and didn't pull it out until a few weeks ago. I somehow knew we would need it on a day like today. Todd Dear, a dear friend of Chuck's, will say a few words and tell the story as Chuck told it to me. (See below.)

Chuck, thank you for letting me tell your story and asking me to walk by your side during these last nine years, especially the last 6 months. Thank you for the members of the community in this room who are connected now because of your spirit. Thank you for the reminders in your last week alive that "to splurge is not a sign of progress" and "live and let live." Thank you for engraining details of this simple recovery program into my mind so I may carry the message through my days.

Chuck, you're wanted in heaven.

I will miss you immensely and love you so deeply.

I will see you on the other side.

CHUCK (2010/2011)
As told to Jill Drader

I was born on April 12, 1932, in St. John, New Brunswick in the general hospital. It was torn down long ago. I was born to Alice Helena Burchill and John Joseph Quilty. They were married. I had two older sisters, but I don't know if they're alive. I lost track of them a few years ago. The oldest one was in St. John N.B., but she died. The oldest was Ann and the next was Francis. I don't know where Francis is, and I don't know if she's alive. Ann was four years older and Francis was two years older. The oldest sister was married to a cop. They had five children. The youngest married a couple of times.

My mom died when I was six months old. She died from a bowel eruption. That's when I was left with my dad. My sisters took care of me to an extent.

For the first four years, we lived on Queen Street in West St. John N.B. When I was four my dad and my uncle (on my mother's side) built a house at 426 City Line, West St. John, N.B. The house is gone. It was torn down in the 1960s. I lived there until I was nineteen or twenty.

My childhood memories are unhappy. I knew I wasn't wanted, and it was made known often. Our relatives lived close by, and they were well off. My sisters had each other for company, so they were ok. I don't think they were wanted either.

My dad remarried Evelyn (Ev) and I had a half-sister. Her name is Julie. I don't know how old she is or where she is. I think she's dead. Maybe 20 years ago. I don't know the cause. She was married and had kids. I don't know anything about them. Maybe two sons. Julie married a guy named Danny Sears. They lived in St. John.

When I was nineteen or twenty, I had a job working as a freight handler in a rail yard on the docks. I joined the army and went to Korea. I thought it was the best thing ever to go to Korea. Because I was in Korea in the war, they kept my job for me. I was in Korea for one year. The army for three total. I loved going back to my freight job, but I was only there ten years before I lost my job due to drinking.

I took a ship to Korea; Simon B. Buckner was the ship. We went to Japan first and then took another ship to Korea. We crossed the international date line on the way there.

On the way back, the ship was called The Patrick. We stayed in the Illusion Islands off Alaska overnight. Then we landed in Seattle and took a tube train home.

Busan was bombed. Bombed out. All of it. Rails curled. The harbour was there. It was 1952. There were no Koreans. The ones we did see were eating garbage. We would go up the side of the hills to sleep. Korea had nice weather. The roads were dusty. We were night fighters. We moved in the dark. We lived in tents and had sea rations. Small canned food. Pasta if anything we cooked. We had coloured cooks (sic). I remember the one cook, he was black from Nova Scotia. He was in Italy in the Second

Appendix

World War. Every day we got free rations of chocolates and American cigarettes. Sometimes shaving cream and full cartons.

When I came back from Korea I had seventy-four days leave. I had a cold for the whole seventy-four days. I spent those seventy-four days in St. John at home. I went hunting and drank rum and beer. I then finished fourteen months in the Army in Valcartier, Quebec. I was with the #5 transport company. They were all French. I didn't get along there much. I didn't speak the language. Every chance I got I drank.

Korea was a good experience. I wouldn't take money for the experience.

I think I was twenty-three when I got out. It was March. In April I was twenty-three. I went back to the docks in West St. John. I was a freight handler. It's where ships came in and out. I stayed there for about ten years. I still lived at #426.

In time, my stepmother put me out. My drinking got worse. I lost my job. My father wanted me to stay. I knew she didn't want me. I was stubborn and knew I was unwanted, so I left.

I stayed in St. John. When I had a place to stay, it was ok. When not, I stayed on the street. I used to get arrested a lot. I went to jail a lot. Mostly for drinking. Sometimes stealing, but not too often. I think I got fourteen or thirty days one time. They knew me in jail, there were only 100,000 people in St. John.

I knew other people in jail. There was one guy I thought had good character. He was a Second World War vet. He was ten years older than me. I saw him on the street once. He was with his sister. I think he had an army pension. We were playing cards in the wing. He had a magazine, and he read the story and showed me the pictures. It was about a boxer in Ireland over 100 years ago, at that time, that's 200 years now. His name was Sir Dan Donnelly. His arms were so long, and he could box in an outside ring. They had his footprints engraved on a racetrack. He died at thirty-three from a Whiskey puke. He lay under a fire hydrant with the water pouring and died that way. He was so dry from drinking alcohol. They dug up his grave, cut off his right arm and had it hung over his bar in a pub, in Ireland. The pub was Byron's in Southern Ireland.

I used to read crime and detective novels in jail. One after the other. The food was poor. Cockroaches. Rats.

I came out west and got a job in a mine, in Manitoba. That was about 1963. They were gold mining. Hard rock. That was alright. I stayed there six months. I wanted to go further West. I worked a bit. Kept drinking. Calgary. Edmonton. Prince George. Kamloops. On the lam.

I liked Edmonton. I sobered up. I had girlfriends. I went to work underground. I worked under the streets of Edmonton putting in water tunnels and runoffs.

I had one girlfriend. She was intelligent. American born. She came to recovery after her husband died. She was well off. Genieve G. They owned a drug store in Camrose one time. At that time, I was working with the commissionaires, for about nine months. She said, "We'll drive to Oshawa and buy a new car there." I said no. I saw the future and it wouldn't work. So, I started drinking again. I was in Edmonton for fourteen years.

There's not too much I was proud of. I was an alcoholic from sixteen years old until I stopped in July 1982.

Then I came to Calgary in July of 1982 and stopped drinking. I went to Renfrew and came out and never drank again. All of a sudden, I wanted to do it for me. And I did it. I never stopped until I wanted to do it for myself. I picked up the big book, read it, and followed it. Paid my rent. I lived on my war veteran's pension at the time.

I moved back to Montreal for a while five years into the program. I lived on 1416 St. Antoine Street over a barber shop owned by two brothers. Italians. The Salvation Army supported me. There were cockroaches everywhere. All over. In the freezer. They would sneak into the fridge. I would wake up and they were on my face and stomach. They are a friend of man. They are. They can kill the black widow.

Facts are stranger than fiction kid, they are.
-Charles Bernard Quilty

Thank Yous

Ms. Baxter, The Divine Miss B, thank you for everything, this whole thing is for you because of you. Thank you for choosing me at 14 years old to start this walk. I miss you. Susan, thank you for hearing her call and for all your support.

This book took a long time to write – thank you for the grace for all the times I said it was ready yet it wasn't. It was never on my timing that the words came through, it was God's time, and with that, the journey was longer and wilder than I ever imagined. Thank you to my family for helping me so much along this way – it takes a village.

I had to eat my own words, take my advice, write back to myself my own prompts, and look hard at my behaviours – over and over. The patterns, spiritual two-hand-shoves, and opportunities to forgive taught me to keep moving forward and showed me over and over how to live in self-forgiveness and with forgiveness.

Artur, there are no words. I'm beyond grateful to continue to walk with your professional practice and truly believe you were called to work with me to learn to heal, differently. This book is a testament to doing the work of your practice. "Looks like we are back to where we started…!" I wouldn't understand PTSD, trauma, anxiety, medications, crashes, and seasons without Dr. Brochu, the Merit IDA team, and you. Thank you.

Tammy Plunkett, thank you for staying on the ride and coming with me to the Pass to learn about The Nest. Then living it. This wouldn't be here without you.

To the writers who supported me through every word of the pain that became this book, thank you. Dana, thank you for answering all my questions. Kim, Jacquelin and LeeAnn – the editing, publishing and distribution agents I wouldn't be here without.

Kate, I would have the cover (or Andy) if it wasn't for that day at the bus stop. I love you. Thanks for holding space for me when I needed someone only like you.

Jen and Jenn, you've kept me upright in your own ways, thank you.

Kristin and Sabrina, you're the only ones who know the whole truth, thank you.

To the men who didn't choose me, thank you.

Tyler, I'm sorry I couldn't do it. Thank you for being the best co-parent I could ask for.

Jake and Coop, I choose you, thank you for choosing me, I love you.

About the Author

Jill Drader is a visionary leader based in Alberta, known for her groundbreaking work in merging logic and intuition through her innovative OwlSeek Method. With a focus on personal and professional development, Jill's unique approach helps individuals tap into their full potential by balancing analytical thinking with intuitive insight. She explores growth, transformation, and self-awareness. A dynamic speaker and educator, Jill empowers people to navigate life's complexities with clarity and confidence, making her a sought-after figure in the realms of personal growth and leadership.

www.ingramcontent.com/pod-product-compliance
Lightning Source LLC
Jackson TN
JSHW022220261224
76063JS00002B/11

* 9 7 8 1 0 6 8 8 9 1 1 0 6 *